♡ Kelsey Hightower

reverb

Published by Student Life Bible Study
A Division of Clarity Publishers

Reverb: Our Lives Echo In The World
©2009 Clarity Publishers

Student Life
Attn: Clarity Publishers
2183 Parkway Lake Drive
Birmingham, AL 35226

Unless otherwise indicated, all Scripture quotations are taken from the Holy Bible:
New International Version (North American Edition), copyright ©1973, 1978, 1984,
by International Bible Society. Used by permission of Zondervan Publishing House.

Some Scripture passages were taken from *The Message*, copyright ©1993, 1994,
1995, 1996, 2000, 2001, 2002. Used by permission of NavPress Publishing Group."

Inside images © jupiterimages, BananaStock, Comstock, Photodisc, istockphoto,
Ruth Tinsley, and Student Life

ISBN-10: 1-935040-14-6
ISBN-13: 978-1-935040-14-9

www.studentlife.com
www.studentlifebiblestudy.com

Printed in the United States of America

reverb

OUR LIVES ECHO IN THE WORLD

Student Life
Birmingham, AL

TABLE OF CONTENTS

How To Use i
Introduction iii

DRIVE: God's Mission in the World 10
Session 1: God's Global Mission 12
Session 2: The Great Commission 18
Session 3: Christ's Commission 24
Session 4: Called and Sent 30
Session 5: The Mission's Cost 36
Session 6: Sharing His Glory 42

STEP OUT: Responding to God's Call 48
Session 1: What Is The Call? 50
Session 2: As You Go 56
Session 3: Without Delay 62
Session 4: Not a Timid Response 68
Session 5: Jonah's Response 74
Session 6: Isaiah's Response 80

THE ANSWER: The Motivating Love of God 86
Session 1: The Source 88
Session 2: Love's Great Sacrifice 94
Session 3: Answering Love 100
Session 4: Vertical Worship 106
Session 5: Vertical Obedience 112
Session 6: Horizontal Living 118

TRANSFER: Disciple Making 101 124
Session 1: Teach By Example 126
Session 2: Testify to the Gospel 132
Session 3: Teaching What is Right 138
Session 4: Serve the World/Love Others 144
Session 5: Do Good to Others 150
Session 6: Show Mercy 156

EMPOWERED: Introducing the Holy Spirit **162**
Session 1: We Have the Power 164
Session 2: Another Helper 170
Session 3: How Can We Know? 176
Session 4: The Big Show 182
Session 5: The Confidence of Certainty 188
Session 6: Guide to Life 194

THE CRUX: Romans and the Gospel **200**
Session 1: Something for Everyone 202
Session 2: Everyone Blows It 208
Session 3: In the Nick of Time 214
Session 4: Getting the Word Out 220
Session 5: The Good Life 226
Session 6: Cause and Effect 232

LIVING LOUD: People Whose Lives Were Heard **238**
Session 1: Moses: Surrender to the mission 240
Session 2: Elijah: On mission in a hostile world 246
Session 3: John the Baptist: On mission regardless of cost 252
Session 4: Nehemiah: Rising to the challenge 258
Session 5: Philip: Anytime, anywhere 264
Session 6: Barnabas: Supporting as we go 270

SQUEEZE: Getting Through the Tough Times **276**
Session 1: The Real Enemy 278
Session 2: The Enemy Within 284
Session 3: Going on the Defense 290
Session 4: Loving the Unlovable 296
Session 5: Push Through It 302
Session 6: More Than Own Our Own 308

Closing **314**
Acknowledgments **316**

HOW TO USE

THE BOOK YOU'RE HOLDING IN YOUR HANDS MAY BE DIFFERENT THAN ANY BOOK YOU'VE EVER HELD.

It is less of a book, and more of an experience.

This book will take you on a journey of discovery . . . A journey that will lead you to answer two very important questions:

What is God's mission and what does it mean to be a part of it?

You will begin to formulate your answers to these questions as you begin to work through the chapters of this book. Each chapter in this book corresponds with a specific 6-week course of StudentLife**Bible**Study's *Reverb* study. These chapters are designed for you to work through at your own pace. From time-to-time your teacher might encourage you to work on specific activities. But for the most part, this book is designed for you to work through on your own.

Told you this book was different . . .

You see, every aspect of this book was designed with **you** in mind.

It is unique. After all, you're unique, too.

There are a lot of different sides to you. The same is true with this book.
There are sections in this book that will challenge you. There are sections that will entertain.

There are activities that will ask you to write down your thoughts, your fears, your dreams ... There are many sections that will ask you merely to think.

The way you encounter this book will depend on the order in which your leader decides to teach you. Some of you will begin this book at the beginning and end at the end. Some of you will start in the middle and jump around. The order you are lead to engage it in doesn't matter as much as your attitude does ...

Your challenge is to commit to reading this book with a teachable spirit. Allow the Holy Spirit to teach and lead you as you are lead to encounter Him. If you approach this book with this attitude, you will find that God will dramatically transform your understanding of Him. He will take you deeper into His presence and begin to use your life in ways you might not be able to imagine right now.

ONE LAST THING AND THIS IS IMPORTANT ... Because this book is unique and made just for you, it works differently than other books. Some pages have activities and instructions. Some pages are thought provoking devotions. Some pages are just pictures meant to stir your mind and heart. The key to using this book is to take every page one at a time, soaking in the content, and letting the Spirit work in your heart.

If at any time you need help, feel free to take the book to your youth leader. Or give us a call at Student Life. We'll be glad to help out.

Reverb

The word *reverb* is short for *reverberate*.

What does it mean to *reverberate*?

To reverberate is to create an echo. God's Word echoes ... It echoes through history and across time. Jesus' life echoes ... The things He did and said still move people today, some 2,000 years later.

Does your life echo? Maybe the better question is, "Does Christ's life and teachings echo through you"?

It's an interesting question. If you want to know the answer, a good start would be to keep reading this book ... **Why should you read this book?** After all, it's big. And it's probably not something you necessarily chose for yourself. Some adult probably encouraged you to give it a shot.

So, what's in it for you? Why is this book worth your time?

Well, believe it or not, this book was designed specifically with teenagers in mind. It was designed with *you* in mind.

What does this mean exactly? Glad you asked ...

This book is **visual**. Quite simply it looks awesome. This was done on purpose. It was done for you. You know what you like. And you don't like dry, stuffy, boring books. So we made this one look really cool.

This book is **interactive**. This book doesn't just tell you stuff, it asks you stuff. There are lots and lots of places for you to share your thoughts, to express yourself, to sound off and give an opinion.

This book is **entertaining**. There are some things that are only included to make you smile. After all, you like to have fun. So a book designed for you should be fun too, right?

But most importantly, this book is **transformative.** Well, maybe it's more like a vehicle of transformation. What does that mean? Well, this book exposes you to God's Word. It points you to His teachings. It introduces you in the most wonderful ways to God and His character.

This book looks cool. It is interactive. It is entertaining. But if it is only those things, it is no different than any magazine on the shelf at your favorite bookstore.

The most important thing about this book is that it brings you into the presence of God the Father, His Son, Jesus, and the Holy Spirit. And it accomplishes all of this by taking you deep into the Word of God, the Bible.

Intrigued? Interested? Curious? Good ...

Keep reading.

This book is made of 8 sections that correspond with the 8, six-week studies you will be studying in class.

Here's a short description of the sessions and what you can expect to find in them.

Session 1—Drive: God's Mission in the World
What is your mission? If you are a Christ-follower, the more important question might be, "What is God's mission"? This section, Drive, is all about understanding God's mission in this world.

Session 2—Step Out: Responding to God's Call
God is at work all around you, all the time. His mission of love and redemption was set in motion when He created the world. Christ calls His followers to join Him on His mission of making disciples of the world. How have you responded?

Session 3—The Answer: The Motivating Love of God
In the culture surrounding you, the very idea of love has been twisted and corrupted. Where do you go to find true, perfect love? The Bible is a great starting point. The Answer brings you face-to-face with the most foundational element in a Christian's life: God's love.

Session 4—Transfer: Disciple Making 101
In His last words to His closest followers, Jesus instructed the disciples to go throughout the world and make disciples. This command should be at the heart of the your mission and purpose.

Session 5—Empowered: Introducing the Holy Spirit
Other than the fact that the Holy Spirit is God, somehow part of the mysterious Trinity, we don't often talk about Him. But God's Spirit is a vital part of our lives as Christ-followers. The Spirit is God's gift of life, truth, and power.

Session 6—The Crux: Romans and the Gospel
When you hear people say the phrase, the Gospel, does it sound old-school to you? Don't be fooled. The Gospel is the heart of God's plan for redeeming His people. If you're looking for how the power of the Gospel works in the world and in the lives of individual believers, the Book of Romans is the place to go.

Session 7—Living Loud: People Whose Lives Were Heard
It is one thing to study the truths of God's mission and purpose. It's another thing to study the powerful stories of biblical people . . . people who dramatically lived out the mission and purpose of God. Living Loud looks at six snapshots from the lives of biblical characters.

Session 8—Squeeze: Getting Through the Tough Times
Let's face it: there are times in life when the going gets pretty tough. You can relate to this, right? Because the world hated Jesus, it will hate you. But, the cool thing is that Jesus won victory over the world. Which means you have, too. But you still have to fight the fight. Which is what Squeeze is all about.

What is your mission? If you are a Christ-follower, the more important question might be, "What is God's mission"? This section, Drive, is all about understanding God's mission. God's mission in this world is pretty profound. God's mission is to reconcile the world to Himself and to make His glory known. Pretty amazing stuff.

You see, God's mission is like a rolling wave, a powerful, majestic force unleashed in the world. The coolest part? God has called us to join His mission . . . . Are you ready to get on board? If you are ready to make God's mission the driving force of your life turn the page . . .

SESSION 1   GOD'S GLOBAL MISSION—Pg 12-17
SESSION 2   THE GREAT COMMISSION—Pg 18-23
SESSION 3   CHRIST'S COMMISSION—Pg 24-29
SESSION 4   CALLED AND SENT—Pg 30-35
SESSION 5   THE MISSION'S COST—Pg 36-41
SESSION 6   SHARING HIS GLORY—Pg 42-47

reverb
reverb
reverb

An ocean wave is unbridled energy in motion. Waves are defined by their inherent and virtually unstoppable power.

Yet, they are a beauty to behold, an awesome blend of grace and force.

GOD'S MISSION IN THIS WORLD IS LIKE AN OCEAN WAVE.

It is always at work. Like a wave, it just is. Waves are constantly in motion, traveling back and forth across the expanses of the ocean. Some we can see. Some we can't. God's mission works in this world like a wave.

AND YOU HAVE A CHOICE.

You can stand on the beach and casually observe as the waves crash all around you.

Detached.

Separated from the work of the wave. Or, you can jump on and soar under its power . . .

Either way, the wave goes on. With or without you, the wave is at work.

Will you watch?

OR WILL YOU RIDE?

THE BLESSING STORY

One of the things we know about God is this: He blesses us with His love and forgiveness. God does this so that through us, His children, He might bless people all over the world.

One way of reading the Bible is to look at it as a huge story of God's plan to bless all people with His love, grace, and mercy. We can actually look at Scripture to see how this story unfolds.

THE BEGINNING . . . READ GENESIS 1:26-28

Humans were always in God's plan. Sin wasn't. But God's plan to redeem people from sin started in the Garden.

CALLING A PEOPLE . . . READ GENESIS 12:1-3

God called Abram to be the father of a great nation. This nation would become the Israelites, or the Jews, and would be the pathway for God's great blessings.

GIVING THE PEOPLE THE LAW . . . READ EXODUS 24:4-8

God gave the Jews His laws so they would live like their Father. The Israelites promised to obey, sealing the promise, or covenant, with blood from a sacrifice.

THE PEOPLE DISOBEY AND ARE PUNISHED . . . READ ISAIAH 1:1-4 AND ISAIAH 5:3-7

God's people turned away from Him and God allowed them to be punished. The nation of Israel was divided in two, and eventually taken over by other nations.

IN THE MIDST OF PUNISHMENT, GOD PROMISED HOPE . . . READ JEREMIAH 23:5-6 AND LUKE 1:26-33

God promised His people He would not leave them, even though they had left Him. He promised to send a king. That King was Jesus, the Son of God, sent to save the world from its sins.

JESUS IS THE WAY TO GOD'S BLESSINGS . . . READ JOHN 14:6 AND EPHESIANS 1:3

Before the world was created, before Adam and Eve, before Abraham . . . Jesus existed. He was God's plan to bring peace, love, mercy, and forgiveness to the world.

So now you know the plotline of God's great story. But the coolest part is that you are part of God's plan, too! You see, God has chosen you, one of His children, to spread the story of Jesus to the world, so that everyone might hear and believe and be blessed.

What are you waiting on? You know the story . . . Who can you tell today?

THE NATIONS KNOW HIM

ESU MFUMU
NTEMWA
I NALIISHIBA.
BANA BONSE E BAKWE,
ANAKA, WENYA KOSA.

CHORUS:
ESU ANTEMWA,
INE ANTEMWA,
ESUS ANTEMWA,
AIBO ANJEBE FI.

CANTONESE

YEHSOU NGOI NGOH,
NGOH HIU DAK
SING SYU GOU NGOH
SAHM MIHNG BAAK
FAAN SIU HAIH JI JYU
MUHK YEUNG
NGOH SEUIH YUHN
YEUHK, JYU GONG
KEUHNG

JYU YEHSOU NGOI NGOH
JYU YEHSOU NGOI NGOH
JYU YEHSOU NGOI NGOH
YAUH SING SYU GOU SOU
NGOH.

ENGLISH

JESUS LOVES ME THIS
I KNOW,
FOR THE BIBLE TELLS
ME SO.
LITTLE ONES TO HIM
BELONG,
THEY ARE WEAK, BUT
HE IS STRONG.

YES, JESUS LOVES ME.
YES, JESUS LOVES ME.
YES, JESUS LOVES ME.
THE BIBLE TELLS ME
SO.

ESPERANTO

JESU-KRISTO
AMAS MIN,
LA BIBLIO
DIRAS GIN;
AL LI
APARTENAS MI,
FEBLAS MI, SED
FORTAS LI.

JES, LI MIN AMAS!
JES, LI MIN AMAS!
JES, LI MIN AMAS!
JESUO AMAS MIN.

ESUS M'AIME! CE
E SAIS
PARCE-QUE LA
BIBLE M'A DIT
LES PETITS UNS A LUI
APARTIENNENT
LS SONT FAIBLES
MAIS IL EST FORT!

UI, JESUS M'AIME
UI, JESUS M'AIME
UI, JESUS M'AIME
LA BIBLE M'A DIT.

GERMAN

JESUS LIEBT MICH
WISSEN WIR,
DENN DIE BIBEL
SAGT ES MIR.
KLEINE KINDER, DIE
SIND SEIN
ER IST STARK UND
SIE SIND REIN.

JA, JESUS LIEBT MICH,
JA, JESUS LIEBT MICH,
JA, JESUS LIEBT MICH,
DIE BIBEL SAGT ES MIR.

HINDI

KYEE SOO MOODJ SAY
KAHR TAH PYAHR
BAI BUHL MAY HAI SAH
MAH CHAR
MAI WHOO(N) NIRH
BAHL WHAH BAHL
WAHN
BAHL COH(N) PUR HAI
THAI UH WAHN

PYAHR KHAR TAH
MOODJ SAY
PYAHR KHAR TAH
MOODJ SAY
PYAHR KHAR TAH
MOODJ SAY
HAI SAH THEE YAH SAH
MAH CHAR

MANDARIN

YEH SU AI WA,
WA TZE TAU
INN YEU SHEN
CH'IN KAU SHU WA
FAN SHIAU HAI
TCHE CHU MUH
YIANG
WA SHUI RUAN
ROKH, CHU KANG
CHIANG

CHU YEH SU AI WA
CHU YEH SU AI WA
CHU YEH SU AI WA
YEU SHEN CH'IN
KAU SHU WA

DEVOTION

SESSION ONE - GOD'S GLOBAL MISSION

If you've had the fortune/curse of putting together a complex piece of furniture (or watched as your mom or dad struggled through it), you know how important the plans are. If you miss even one step, the whole thing may fall apart. There's nothing more frustrating than getting to the end of a project only to find you put something on backwards or upside down.

The stakes are higher if you help another person put something together. Not only do you have to make sure you're both on the same page, there's the added pressure of building something for someone else. You want to make sure you do a good job so they will be happy with their new creation.

READ PSALM 67:1–7. While we don't actually know who wrote this psalm, it's safe to say they were thankful for God's blessing. This psalm seems to be more of a prayer than a hymn. And while songs or prayers like this were usually sung after successful harvests, this psalm has a deeper message.

Go read verse 1 again and think to yourself how you might summarize it in one sentence. A good summary might read something like, "The psalmist is praying for God's good favor, or blessing." Simple enough. Now here's the cool part. Read verse 2 and, again, think how you might summarize it in one sentence. You might have come up with something similar to, "The psalmist wants all the people of the world to know of God and His ways." Put these two verses together and an awesome picture appears.

The psalmist wants God to bless him and his people. But this petition for blessing is not out of a selfish desire. It's so that others might see the blessings God has poured out, give God glory for these blessings, and desire to be similarly blessed. The goal of the psalmist's prayer is so God would be glorified.

When you build a piece of furniture or fix a bike, you have to follow a plan. A set of rules. A guide that has the big picture in mind. God's mission to reach the world is the same way. He has a plan. And the coolest part is that you play a major role in His plan. He has chosen you, your friends, your church, and all Christ-followers everywhere to be one of the main ways God spreads HIS story of love, grace, and redemption. Do you take this responsibility seriously? Do you live in such a way that your life follows God's plan to share His love with all the world? What changes do you need to make today in order to be on mission with God in all that you do?

GOD'S MISSION IS ADVANCING
THE BEGINNING

God's mission is to bless His people, so through them,
He can bless all nations. This mission started in the Garden of Eden.

Where: We don't know exactly where Eden was, but many scholars believe that it could have been near the convergence of the Tigris and Euphrates Rivers.

When: There is a lot of debate about exactly when God created the Universe. The most important thing for you to know is that God was the Creator. When He did the creating is not near as essential.

THEREFORE, GO AND
DISCIPLES OF ALL NAT
THEM IN THE NAME OF
OF THE SON AND
SPIRIT, AND TEAC
EVERYTHING I HAVE
AND SURELY I AM
ALWAYS, TO THE
- MATTHEW 28:18-20

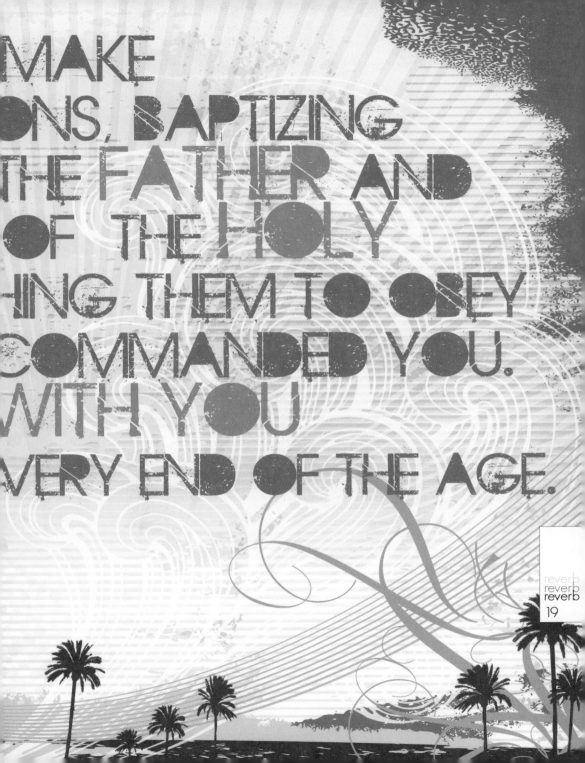

THE HEART
OF JESUS' GREAT COMMISSION

You've probably heard before that the New Testament you have in your Bible was originally translated from manuscripts written in Greek. This is cool for two reasons:
You don't have to learn Greek (or Hebrew, or Latin) to read the Bible.
We can look back at some of the original Greek words and sometimes gain a deeper meaning to a specific verse or passage.

You're going to get a chance to look at the original Greek wording of a familiar passage. The new emphasis you uncover might just really open your eyes to your role in God's mission.

Are you familiar with The Great Commission? TURN TO MATTHEW 28. Start reading with verse 18 and read to verse 20. You've read this before, right? It's an important passage. One bible scholar has even called it the key to understanding the entire Gospel!

So, here's the question: Do you really understand it? Do you really get what Jesus was saying to His disciples LET'S TAKE A CLOSER LOOK AT VERSE 19. Look at the verse and identify the word you think is the key word, th most important word in the passage.

Which word did you choose? Did you choose "go"? If so, don't feel bad. A lot of people use the Grea Commission as motivation for traveling to go on mission trips. And that's OK. Jesus definitely calls u to leave our comfort zones to tell the world about Him. But the word "go" is not the main focus o the command.

THE KEY WORD IN THE SENTENCE IS REALLY THE PHRASE "MAKE DISCIPLES."

This is where a good knowledge of Greek comes in. The Greek wor mathetuo is what's called an "imperative verb." An imperative verb i used to give orders or commands. So when we read Matthew 28:19 we should look at the phrase "make disciples" as the command, no the word "go."

NOW DO YOU GET IT?

How does the meaning of the Great Commission change i Jesus is not necessarily putting the emphasis on the "going, but instead is emphasizing "making disciples"? How doe this change the way you are living your day-to-day life fo Christ?

READ VERSE 20. Jesus gives a big clue into how we ar supposed to make disciples. What does He say we are t do? What does He say about the power we will have t teach people about Him?

Now that you know what you are called to do, what's keepin you from doing it? How are you going to join God on His missio of making disciples for Christ?

Try the all new
Mission Goggles

Guaranteed to open your eyes to God's mission in the world

Tired of wondering what God's plan is for your life? Sick of missing opportunities to make a difference? Well, here's your chance to do something about it!

Try Mission Goggles! Everything looks different through these amazing glasses!

Just place Mission Goggles on, adjust the Sure-Fit nosepieces, and BANG! All of the sudden the world looks different! The secret is the revolutionary technology that enables you to see the world exactly as God does!

In no time you'll see that God is working all around you to accomplish His mission and purposes. You'll begin to view even the most familiar places as opportunities to make a difference for Christ. When you look at people through Mission Goggles you'll begin to see them as God does. You'll notice that each person has value! Each person is worthy of God's love!

Don't delay! Order your Mission Goggles today!

See the world exactly as God does!

DEVOTION

Do you see him over there? The old man by the trashcan with his head resting against the wall. See him? No ... don't bother him; he's sleeping. Just watch. Watch what's about to happen . . .

See that woman walking towards him? The one on her cell phone? Yeah, her. She walks past here every morning. And he's usually there. The truth is that she's not really on her cell phone. She's faking it so she doesn't have to look at him. When he asks her for change or for food it makes her so uncomfortable. So today she's pretending to talk on her phone so he won't bother her.

Now, look again. See the teenaged girl with the torn jeans coming this way? Her name's Cassie. She's pretty, don't you think? Well, the truth about Cassie's life isn't pretty at all. Her dad's a drunk. He took-off a couple of years ago. Her mom works so much Cassie hardly sees her. Most days Cassie's barely holding it together, herself. But watch what she does as she nears the old man. See her reaching into her bag? She's pulling out a blanket she brought from home. See, she passed by the old man yesterday and noticed he was shivering. So today she brought him a blanket.

See how she drapes it over him? Soft, so as not to wake him. Watch her lift his hand and put it under the blanket so he'll be warmer. See how she stares at him before she walks off? Makes you wonder what she is thinking . . .

What if I told you she was praying? She prays for him a lot, actually. She doesn't know his name. He doesn't know her either. But she prays for him. She prays that God would keep him safe. That he would know someone cares for him. That he would know Jesus cares for him. That he would know she cares for him.

And there goes Cassie . . . Off to who knows where.

Cassie doesn't have all the answers. And she doesn't make all the right choices. But she tries. And she cares. She cares for the lost, the sick, the lonely, the outcast, the broken-hearted. Cassie cares for those forgotten.

Why?

Because she loves Jesus. And Jesus cares for the forgotten, too.

Jesus went through all the towns and villages, teaching in their synagogues, preaching the good news of the kingdom and healing every disease and sickness. When he saw the crowds, he had compassion on them, because they were harassed and helpless, like sheep without a shepherd. Then he said to his disciples, "The harvest is plentiful but the workers are few. Ask the Lord of the harvest, therefore, to send out workers into his harvest field."
—Matthew 9:35-38

GOD'S MISSION IS ADVANCING
COMMISSION ACCEPTED

The Great Commission is the ultimate expression of Christ's call to embrace the purpose of God and to declare His glory to all nations.

WHERE: God's desire is for all people everywhere to know Him and His love for them. The cool thing about this map is that it shows just how far the message of Christ had spread during the 1st Century.

WHEN: Think about how far the story of Christ had spread in such a short amount of time. There was no phone, no Internet, no way of mass communication. Jesus' amazing plan for His creation spread by word-of-mouth. The cool thing is that it is still spread that way today. When was the last time you told someone Jesus' story?

WATER...

It's a simple element.
Yet it's central to life as we know it.

Our earth would not be sustainable without water.

Plant and animal life would cease.

Oceans and forests would become deserts.

No lakes and streams.

No waterfalls.

No raindrops.

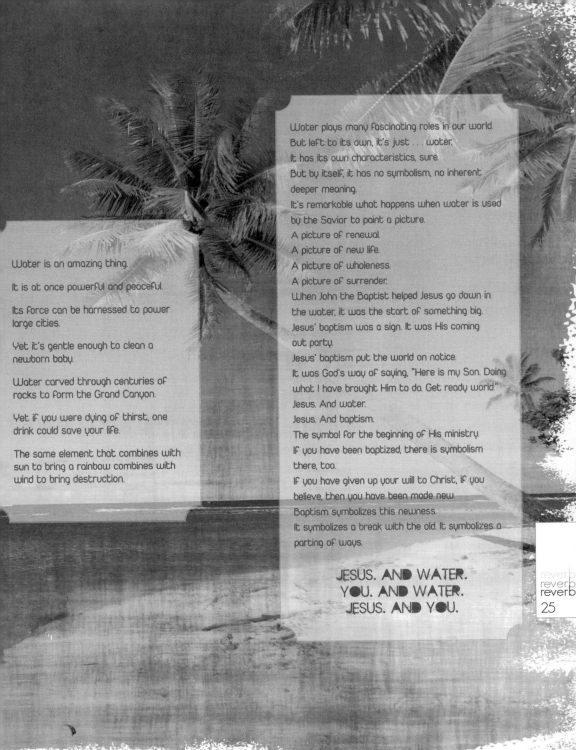

Water is an amazing thing.

It is at once powerful and peaceful.

Its force can be harnessed to power large cities.

Yet it's gentle enough to clean a newborn baby.

Water carved through centuries of rocks to form the Grand Canyon.

Yet if you were dying of thirst, one drink could save your life.

The same element that combines with sun to bring a rainbow combines with wind to bring destruction.

Water plays many fascinating roles in our world. But left to its own, it's just . . . water. It has its own characteristics, sure. But by itself, it has no symbolism, no inherent deeper meaning. It's remarkable what happens when water is used by the Savior to paint a picture. A picture of renewal. A picture of new life. A picture of wholeness. A picture of surrender. When John the Baptist helped Jesus go down in the water, it was the start of something big. Jesus' baptism was a sign. It was His coming out party. Jesus' baptism put the world on notice. It was God's way of saying, "Here is my Son. Doing what I have brought Him to do. Get ready world." Jesus. And water. Jesus. And baptism. The symbol for the beginning of His ministry. If you have been baptized, there is symbolism there, too. If you have given up your will to Christ, if you believe, then you have been made new. Baptism symbolizes this newness. It symbolizes a break with the old. It symbolizes a parting of ways.

JESUS. AND WATER.
YOU. AND WATER.
JESUS. AND YOU.

BURIED WITH JESUS??

What does it mean to be baptized? Let's take a closer look through one of the Apostle Paul's letters. Grab your Bible and flip to the Book of Romans. Turn to chapter six. Now take a quick break from all that hard work. Let's pause for a second and set the stage.

Paul was writing to the Christians in Rome. Back before Facebook™ walls, people would write letters. Paul wrote letters to specific churches, churches in a general region, or in the case of Romans, the Christ-followers in the city of Rome. These letters Paul wrote would be read aloud, copied, and passed around to different bodies of believers throughout the region. It's amazing to think that you are reading a letter sent thousands of years ago.

Now, back to Romans chapter 6. Take a minute and read verses 1-4. In verse 1, Paul is defending himself against a common put-down used by his enemies. His enemies accused him of saying that God has so much grace, we should just keep sinning so He gets a chance to use it on us. Paul is saying, "Of course I'm not saying that"!

Read verse 2. In your own words, what do you think Paul means when he said, "we died to sin"?

If you have submitted your life to Jesus' lordship, if you have told Him you believe in Him, then you have been given a new life. Your old life was characterized by sin's power over you. Your new life, the life purchased for you by Jesus' death on the cross, is a life characterized by freedom from sin. You literally have died to sin's power.

Now read verses 3 and 4. In biblical times, baptisms were done by completely submerging an individual under water, then bringing them back up. (Many churches still follow this practice today. Your church may or may not practice submersion.) Describe how being submerged under the water is a picture of being buried.

Describe how being raised out of the water is a picture of Christ's being raised from the dead.

Baptism itself doesn't take away sin's power over you. But it is a beautiful symbol of your new life in Christ.

If you have more questions about baptism, talk to an adult in your church about how baptism is practiced in your church.

YOUR MISSION NOW

You're about halfway through this section on God's mission. In your own words, write down a one-sentence definition of what God's mission is.

Done? Good . . . Now here's another question for you. When you think about being involved in God's mission, what is the first thing that comes to mind? For many people the answer to this question will be some sort of mission trip, or other mission project. Is this what you thought of?

Going on mission trips is awesome, no doubt. But your involvement in God's mission is intended to be so much more than just formal mission trips with your church.

YOU ARE CALLED TO BE INVOLVED WITH GOD'S MISSION TODAY. RIGHT WHERE YOU ARE. IN YOUR HOME. YOUR SCHOOL. AND YOUR COMMUNITY.

Here's a challenge for you. Think about the opportunities you will be presented with in the next day. Write down a few ways you can make a difference for Jesus in your world sometime in the next 24 hours.

Don't stop there. Think about the things God has gifted you with. Your talents. Your passions. Your desires. Your interests. List some ideas for using your gifts to make a difference for Christ in your community. Think in terms of how you can make a difference in the next few weeks or months.

Now, go one step further. Write a prayer in the space below. Ask God to reveal to you how He wants to use you to make a difference in the life of someone far away from where you live. Keep praying for this until God answers you. Who knows where HE might lead!

reverb
reverb
reverb
27

DEVOTION

SESSION THREE - CHRIST'S COMMISSION

Chances are, if you're reading this you're a teenager. And if you're a teenager, you're actually in a pretty cool time of your life. While it's hard to see it now, you are doing things that will shape your future, long after your teenage years are over. Many of the decisions you make in the next few years will affect the path you choose after high school, which, in most cases, affects your career, who you will marry, where you will live . . . Big decisions, right?

The coolest thing is that you will reach a point, years down the road, when you can look back and identify the truly important moments in your life. You will be able to point to two or three moments as the ones that really jump-started the process of shaping the person you will have become.

Believe it or not, Jesus had one of these moments. STOP FOR A MOMENT AND READ MATTHEW 3:11-17. This passage is Matthew's version of Jesus' baptism. At the beginning, you see John the Baptist talking about the coming Messiah, God's Son who will take away the sins of the world. All of a sudden, Jesus is on the scene. John realizes Jesus is the promised Messiah. While John is initially hesitant to baptize Jesus, he agrees and Jesus is baptized.

Go back and read verses 16 and 17 again. This is the reason God desired for Jesus to be baptized. Most people in John's day were baptized as a way of symbolizing their repentance from sin. Jesus was perfect, therefore He did not need to symbolize repentance. So why be baptized? Verses 16 and 17 tell us. Jesus' baptism was God's way of showing the world that the time of Jesus' ministry had begun.

Notice the two things that happened: the Holy Spirit descended on Jesus, anointing Him for God's work. And, God validated Jesus' identity and mission by audibly recognizing Jesus as His Son. So, as we look back at Jesus' life and ministry, His baptism was one of those monumentally important moments that shaped His life to come. Looking back, it was the start of His true purpose and mission on this earth.

You will have these moments, too. Moments where God uses you. Moments you will look back on and realize how important they were to your overall spiritual development.

The real question is, will you be ready when your moment comes?

GOD'S MISSION IS ADVANCING
GOD'S MISSION IN YOUR COMMUNITY

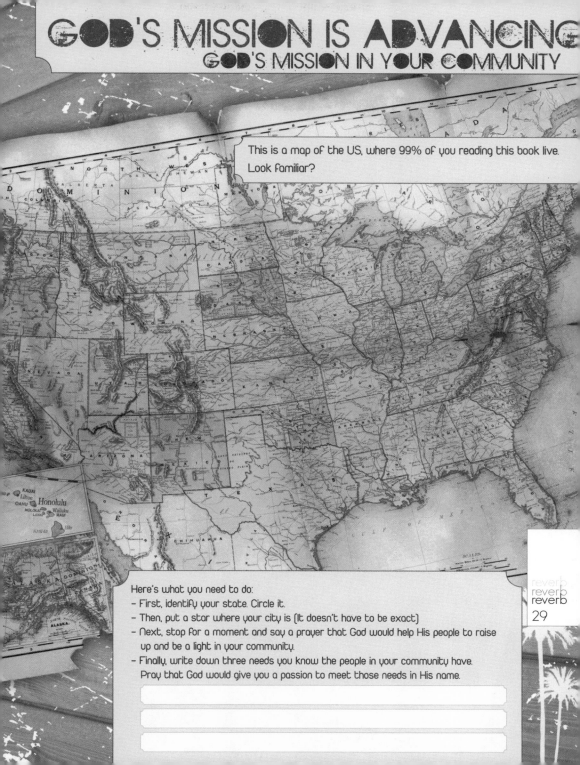

This is a map of the US, where 99% of you reading this book live. Look familiar?

Here's what you need to do:
- First, identify your state. Circle it.
- Then, put a star where your city is (It doesn't have to be exact)
- Next, stop for a moment and say a prayer that God would help His people to raise up and be a light in your community.
- Finally, write down three needs you know the people in your community have. Pray that God would give you a passion to meet those needs in His name.

FRIENDS

FAMILY

04341077087-8

sus called you to follow Him. But He doesn't expect you
merely follow . . . He expects you to join Him in His
ssion to **save the world.**

ok at the following categories. In the space under the photo,
rite how you can be on mission for God with the particular
oup of people shown.

By now, you probably have a pretty good idea of what we're talking about in this section, right? We're talking about God's call on your life.

We've said that phrase a lot, haven't we?

"GOD'S CALL"

Hopefully you've begun to grasp the deeper meaning of this phrase. Hopefully you've learned that God calls all believers to join His mission. And His mission is huge! By this point you've started to understand that God's plan for redeeming humankind has been in motion since Creation. In fact, you might say that God created the world with His plan in mind. From day one, God knew His mission was to call to Himself a people who would honor and glorify Him with their lives. From the beginning, God knew He would set in place a plan that allowed His people to draw close to Him, in spite of their sinfulness flying in the face of His perfect righteousness.

You are called to be on this mission.

But there's more . . .

PAUSE FOR A MOMENT AND READ LUKE 9:1-6 AND LUKE 10:1-2. Circle the groups of people Jesus sent out. You'll notice two groups of people: the Twelve (Jesus' closest disciples) and the 72 (a larger group of Jesus' followers). Both of these groups of people had committed to following Jesus. He was their teacher. And at least some, if not most, believed or otherwise sensed that Jesus was indeed the Son of God. In other words, these folks were on-board. They understood the mission and had signed up. They knew they were called.

But Jesus didn't let them just follow Him around. In this passage, we see Jesus sending them out to make a difference in God's name. Jesus gave them power to heal and authority to preach about God's Kingdom. His followers were called. And they were sent.

Jesus desires the same for you. He has called you to be a part of His plan to reconcile all people to Him. But Jesus' desire is that you would boldly live your life for Him, telling people about Him in your words and actions, as His representatives on this earth.

Do you accept the call? Will you live your life as one sent by Christ? Don't waste the chance to impact this world in Jesus' name.

reverb
reverb
reverb
32

LIVING OUT THE CALL

How willing are you to allow God to send you out? It's easy to think about going overseas or to another country. That's pretty exotic, right? And, it's easy to share with people you'll most likely never see again.

But how willing are you to go out into your community in the name of Jesus and share His message of love and forgiveness? (Ouch.... Did that hit too close to home?)

Take a moment and list two or three areas in your community where people could use a fresh reminder of God's love for them.

But don't stop there.... Take a minute and brainstorm some ideas for ways you could be a part of bringing God's message to that community.

You've come too far to stop now.... Commit to talking with your youth leader about what your youth group can do to make some of your ideas come to life.

YOU KNOW YOU HAVE BEEN CALLED. AND YOU KNOW GOD WANTS TO SEND YOU AND YOUR FRIENDS TO GO AND MAKE A DIFFERENCE IN HIS NAME. DO NOT LET THIS OPPORTUNITY PASS BY YOU. BE A PART OF GOD'S MISSION IN YOUR WORLD TODAY!

DEVOTION

SESSION FOUR - CALLED AND SENT

When you think about "being sent" by God on mission with Him, what do you think about? Do you think about missionaries working in far away exotic places? Do you think about people who leave their careers to start churches? Do you think about short-term mission trips like the ones your youth group probably takes? While these are certainly all examples of being sent, it's important for you to understand that being sent out on mission with God doesn't just mean moving to another country or planting churches.

There's more to being called and sent out than organized mission experiences. You can be sent out in the simplest of ways. For example . . .

Take a second and read Acts 7:57–8:4. Now, you are picking up at the end of a long story. Stephen, a member of the early Jerusalem Church and a Christ-follower, was testifying to the true identity of Jesus before one of the Jewish courts. The Jews were so furious at Stephen for claiming Jesus was the Son of God that they dragged Stephen out and killed him. That's what you read about in verse 57. Stephen boldly spoke the truth about Christ no matter the cost. But that's not where I want you to pay attention.

Focus on Acts 8:4. Paul and the other anti-Christian Jews were running these Christ-followers out of Jerusalem. Yet, verse 4 gives us a glimpse of the character in these individuals. These followers of Christ didn't allow persecution to keep them from carrying out God's mission. As they were forced out of Jerusalem, they continued to share with others about all Jesus was doing. That's pretty amazing, isn't it?

These believers found themselves in a circumstance they could not control. You probably find yourself in these types of situations often. After all, you don't have a lot of choice about going to school, do you? While you're there, why don't you treat your school like a mission experience? Consider what it looks like to be called by God and sent to your school as a light for God's Kingdom.

You don't have to go to a far away country. The biggest opportunity you have is right in front of you each and every day. Don't miss your chance!

GOD'S MISSION IS ADVANCING
THE RESULTS OF BEING CALLED AND SENT

This map is a very rough model of the spread of world religions. While it is not exact, it will give you a really good idea of where Christianity is strong . . . and where it is not.

As you look at this map, what do you see?

If you just see a map with a bunch of countries, you might want to pray that God would begin to soften your heart to the plight of those who do not know Christ.

On the other hand, if you look at this map and see an opportunity to go and spread the story of Jesus, then your heart is in the right spot. Pray that God would give you the strength to going wherever His call sends you.

Roman Catholic
Protestant
Eastern Orthodox
Muslim
Buddhist
Hinduism
Animism

THE MAN WHO LOVES HIS

LOSE IT, WHILE THE MAN W

HIS LIFE IN THIS WORLD WI

ETERNAL LIFE. WHOEVER

SERVES ME MUST FOLLOW

ME; AND WHERE I AM, M

SERVANT ALSO WILL BE. M

FATHER WILL HONOR TH

ONE WHO SERVES ME

LIFE WILL
O HATES
EEP IT FOR

JOHN 12:25-26

DEVOTION

SESSION FIVE - THE MISSION'S COST

Take a moment and think about the answer to the following questions:

WHAT DO YOU HOLD MOST DEARLY? WHAT IS THE ONE THING YOU VALUE ABOVE ALL ELSE? WHAT IS THE ONE SPECIFIC THING YOU HOLD ON TO MOST?

Don't move on without stopping for a moment and thinking about your answer.

Got it? How did you respond? Did your answer take the form of an object, such as your iPhone, your electric guitar, your laptop, or your car? Or maybe your answer took the form of a relationship; maybe the thing you value the most is your parent or parents, your siblings, or maybe even your best friend. However you responded, hopefully you were able to think of one thing you particularly value above all else.

Your answer to the question "What do you hold most dearly?" actually reveals a lot about your priorities. It may not seem like it at first, but your answer says a lot about how you view the world. Keep that thought in mind as we pause for a moment. . . .

Stop and read John 12:23–26. Jesus was in Jerusalem for a special celebration called the Passover Feast. The Passover celebrated the Lord delivering the Jews from slavery in Egypt. Shortly before this passage, Jesus' followers had heaped praises on Him as He entered the city. Yet, Jesus knew His time was drawing to an end. In this passage, Jesus' words let us know that He knew exactly the sacrifice He would soon make on the cross.

Look back at verses 25–26. Jesus basically says we cannot follow Him if the thing we hold most dear is our own life. Jesus is helping His followers (and that includes you) understand that their lives should be totally committed to God. Literally! You should view your life as if it belonged to God. You should treat your life as something that is to be given over, sacrificed for God to use and direct in order to draw glory to Himself.

You cannot follow God if you hold too dearly to this life. To be the greatest credit to God's Kingdom you should view your relationship with Christ as most important, above all else in your life. Only then will you be able to fully embrace your role as a part of His mission.

How can you begin to let go of your life, giving yourself over to God to be used as He sees fit?

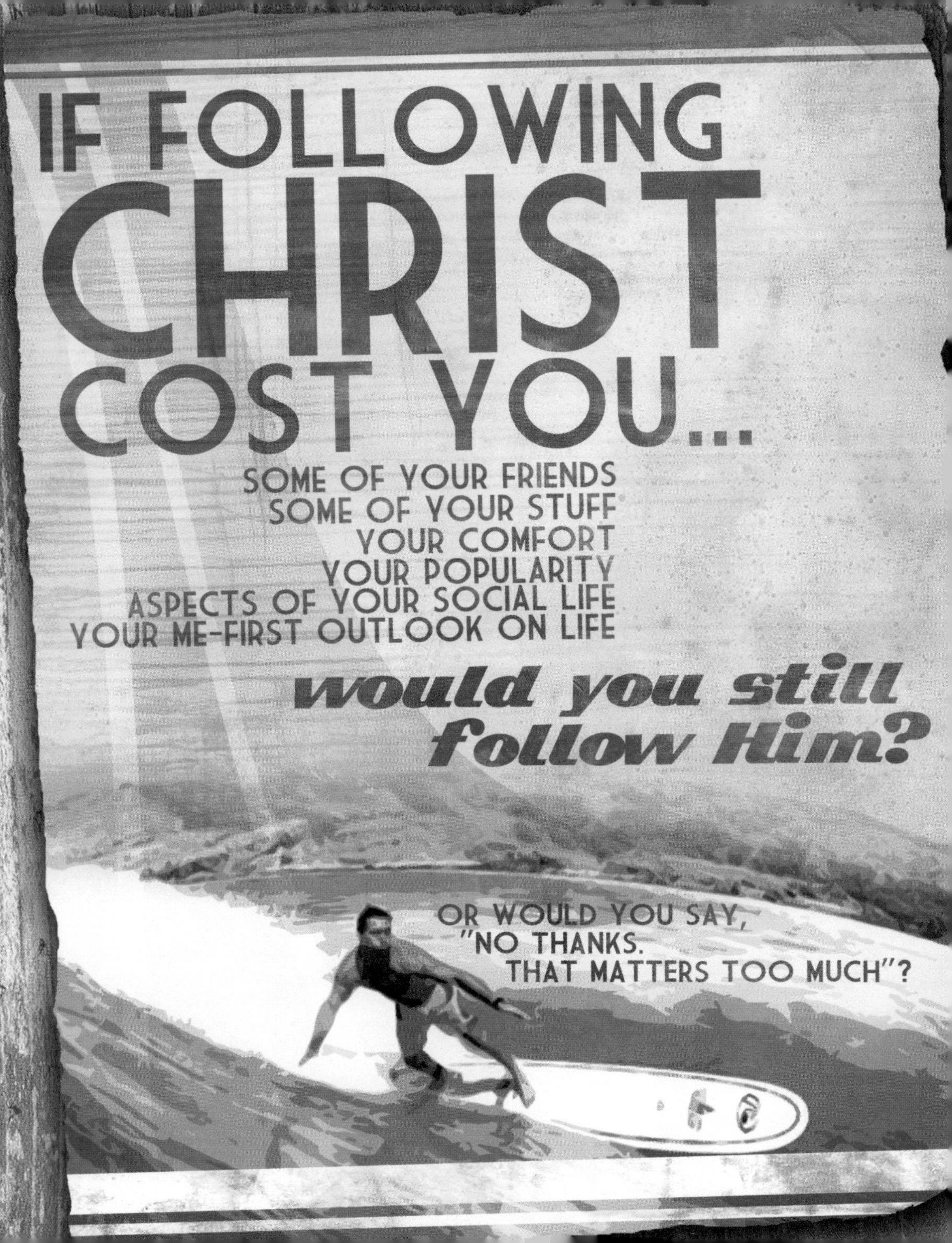
IF FOLLOWING
CHRIST
COST YOU...
SOME OF YOUR FRIENDS
SOME OF YOUR STUFF
YOUR COMFORT
YOUR POPULARITY
ASPECTS OF YOUR SOCIAL LIFE
YOUR ME-FIRST OUTLOOK ON LIFE
would you still
follow Him?
OR WOULD YOU SAY,
"NO THANKS.
THAT MATTERS TOO MUCH"?

Let's be clear about one thing: God's plan calls for us humans to play a major part in spreading His message of love to the whole world. Deep down inside, you might not feel comfortable with this. If you are honest with yourself, the thought of being an important part of God's plan might scare you a bit. But regardless of what you might have been taught or what you think you know, you should probably get one thing straight up front:

If you choose not to live your life as a part of God's mission, you are failing. You are failing to live up to what God has planned for your life.

This truth might seem harsh to you. But that doesn't make it any less true. If you claim to believe in Jesus Christ, you can NOT refuse to accept His call to be on mission. Jesus doesn't give us that option.

You were meant to live life boldly on mission for God. And if you commit to living this way, there will be a cost.

In fact, there will be a cost on the front end. Simply by deciding to let God use your life for His purposes, you will have to say "no" to some things.

Take a moment and answer the following questions. Be honest! This is an opportunity for you to really think about your life.

Do you have things in your life—for example, material things, selfish desires, or even people—standing in the way of you telling God that He can use your life however He wants?

List any of those things below. (If you don't want to write these out, use an abbreviation, initials, or some other symbol that only you will recognize.)

If you know something has come between you and God, then what is keeping you from deciding to follow God no matter the cost?

Do you feel the Spirit nudging you to make the tough decisions you need to make in order to fully give your life to God? Don't waste anymore time! Pray right now that God would give you the strength to make the choices you need to make in order to follow Him. If you want, write your prayer below:

GOD'S MISSION IS ADVANCING
THE 10/40 WINDOW

Have you ever heard of the 10/40 Window?

The 10/40 Window is an area that contains the highest population of non-Christians in the world. It's called the 10/40 Window because it is all the land from 10 degrees to 40 degrees North of the equator. Its eastern and western boundaries are North Africa and China. Statistics show that literally hundreds of millions of people living there have either never heard or never believed in the name of Christ.

Men and women who have committed to telling these people about Jesus do so at a great risk to themselves. Most of these areas are hostile to Christians. Why do you think these people are so willing to sacrifice everything for God to use them to reach the 10/40 Window?

Pray for the people in the 10/40 Window, as well as the Christ-followers who willingly sacrifice all to reach them for Christ.

GOD'S CHARACTERISTICS

LOVING

EVER-PRESENT

MERCIFUL

RIGHTEOUS

COMPASSIONATE

JUST

ALL-KNOWING GRACIOUS MIGHTY AWE-INSPIRING HOLY UNCHANGING

OK . . . Let's see how well you know this stuff.

In your own words, write how you would explain "God's glory" to someone who has never heard of God and never gone to church. (This is a hard one. But really, give it a shot and see what you come up with.)

_____

_____

_____

_____

Now that you have had some time to think about it, here's a little help at a definition:

GOD'S GLORY IS ALL THAT GOD IS—HIS CHARACTERISTICS, HIS NATURE, AND HIS PERSON. IT IS THE TOTAL SUM OF EVERYTHING THAT MAKES GOD, WELL, GOD.

Now here's a confession: even the above definition is not perfect. You see, it is difficult to define God's glory in just a few words. So, here's a little more:

In the Old Testament, God's glory was almost always associated with His presence. So, when God appeared to Moses in the burning bush or to the priests in the Tabernacle, it was said that His glory was revealed. (By the way, this scared the heck out of the Israelites . . . and rightly so! You'd be scared too if God appeared in front of you!)

In the New Testament the idea of God revealing Himself still remained. But in many ways, this took the form of the revelation of Himself through His Son, Jesus. Think about the events surrounding Jesus' life: the angels appearing to the shepherds; Jesus' baptism; Jesus' transfiguration in front of Peter, James, and John; and Jesus' death and resurrection. These are all powerful examples of God's glory demonstrated through His Son, Jesus.

So, God's glory is more or less the revealing of Himself in all of His wonder.

Another question: What is the primary way God reveals Himself to you, a modern day follower of Christ?

_____

If you answered the Bible, you're correct! (Nice job, BTW . . .)

As we've been talking about God's mission, you've probably gathered by now that you play an important part. You have been chosen as a messenger of God's glory! The goal is for your life to be all about making God's glory known in your world.

PRACTICAL GUIDE TO SHARING GOD'S GLORY

Read the following scenarios. For each scenario there are several ways you might share God's glory. For each, circle the answer you would feel most comfortable trying.

SCENARIO 1

Today you found out a girl in your grade is pregnant. As you leave practice, you see her sitting alone. She has her head in her hands, crying. In this situation, how can you be a messenger of God's glory?

HOW WOULD YOU RESPOND?

1. Share with her that God is a God of forgiveness.
2. Help her see that He is always there when we need Him.
3. Explain that even if she feels abandoned, God will always love her.

SCENARIO 2

Your best friend just found out he/she got accepted to the college you both wanted to attend. You however, you did not. In this situation, how can you be a messenger of God's glory?

HOW WOULD YOU RESPOND?

1. Express comfort in the fact that God is all-knowing and has a perfect plan.
2. Confess your disappointment but explain that you know God is compassionate and will ease your pain.
3. Make it known that since God is unchanging, you can have confidence that He will be with you through any trial.

SCENARIO 3

You find yourself in a discussion with a guy at school whom you know is an atheist. He says he doesn't like Christians because they're all hypocrites. In this situation, how can you be a messenger of God's glory?

HOW WOULD YOU RESPOND?

1. Agree that sure, people are imperfect, but then help him see that God is perfect.
2. Explain that you believe God is truth. Encourage him to seek out God's truth in the Bible and see what God says.
3. Express how Jesus' love and mercy saved your life. Encourage him to allow Jesus a chance to do the same thing in his life.

SCENARIO 4

Your best friend just found out his/her dad has been having an affair. He/she is hurt and angry and has turned to you for your help. In this situation, how can you be a messenger of God's glory?

HOW WOULD YOU RESPOND?

Come up with your own answer.

DEVOTION

SESSION SIX - SHARING HIS GLORY

What's the difference between the burrito at your favorite Mexican restaurant and the shady microwaveable ones you buy by the bag-full from the freezer section of your local grocery store? It's the same exact difference between a feature length movie released in theatres and a bootlegged version downloaded from the Web. There's just something different about the real thing, isn't there?

More often than not, the authentic, original article is worth the extra money, time, or energy that separates it from a knock-off variety. Whether it's clothes, cars, or food, the real thing earns our praise while the sub-par versions usually serve as a punch line in a joke.

God is the same way. What? Seriously . . . Keep reading.

Read Psalm 96:1-13. It immediately becomes obvious that this psalm is an amazing testimony of praise to God. The Israelites lived in a world much like ours in at least one significant way: They were surrounded by a culture that embraced multiple gods and religions. So, in a way, the psalmist was saying that God was worthy to be praised because He is the real thing! Not some imposter, God really is "the God who made the heavens." God is righteous and will judge the nations. Because of this, the psalmist says He is "most worthy of praise" (v. 4).

Part of following Christ is living your life in such a way that you are constantly giving praise to God. Your actions, words, inner thoughts, and outward emotions should reflect a worldview that is influenced by your love for God and for His Son. When you live this way, you will actually lead others to recognize God's greatness.

Your life can be a testimony to God's glory. After all, He's the real deal, worth every bit of your praise and service.

GOD'S MISSION IS ADVANCING

PRAYER MAP

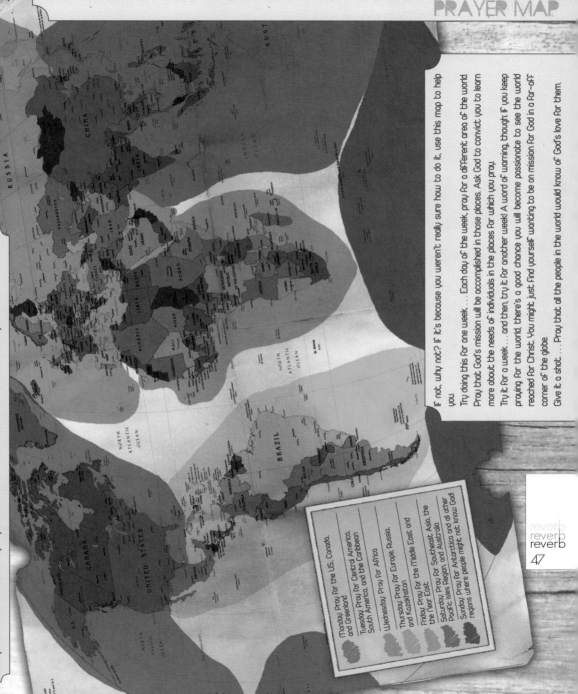

IF not, why not? IF it's because you weren't really sure how to do it, use this map to help you.

Try doing this for one week... Each day of the week, pray for a different area of the world. Pray that God's mission will be accomplished in those places. Ask God to convict you to learn more about the needs of individuals in the places for which you pray.

Try it for a week... and then, try it for another week! A word of warning, though: If you keep praying for the world, there's a good chance you will become passionate to see the world reached for Christ. You might just find yourself wanting to be on mission for God in a far-off corner of the globe.

Give it a shot.... Pray that all the people in the world would know of God's love for them.

Monday: Pray for the US, Canada, and Greenland

Tuesday: Pray for Central America, South America, and the Caribbean

Wednesday: Pray for Africa

Thursday: Pray for Europe, Russia, and Kazakhstan

Friday: Pray for the Middle East and the Near East

Saturday: Pray for Southeast Asia, the Pacific Isles Region, and Australia

Sunday: Pray for Antarctica and all other regions where people might not know God!

reverb
reverb
reverb
47

WHAM!

God is at work all around you, all the time. His mission of love and redemption was set in motion when He created the world. Yet, His mission is just as real and alive today as it was during biblical times. Do you claim to be a Christ-follower? If so, you have a decision to make: Will you step out and be on mission with Him? Or will you sit on the sidelines as the mission passes you by?

Christ calls His followers to join Him on His mission of making disciples of the world. Joining Him will cost you, a fact Christ Himself recognized. However, Jesus desires nothing less than a bold, immediate, and positive response. How have you responded? God allows us to work alongside Him. Will you step out?

Session 1: What Is The Call?—Pg 50-55

Session 2: As You Go—Pg 56-61

Session 3: Without Delay—Pg 62-67

Session 4: Not a Timid Response—Pg 68-73

Session 5: Jonah's Response—Pg 74-79

Session 6: Isaiah's Response—Pg 80-85

SACrifice!

Then Jesus said to his disciples, "If anyone would come after me, he must deny himself and take up his cross and follow me."
— Matthew 16:24

hmmm... what does "take up his cross" mean?

"... and you will be my witnesses in Jerusalem, and in all Judea and Samaria, and to the ends of the earth."
— Acts 1:8

I believe in God
I believe Jesus was His Son
But do I really follow Jesus?

Dale Earnhardt Jr. Richard "Rip" Hamilton. LeBron James. What do these celebrities have in common? Each of these athletes surrounds himself with a tight-knit circle of followers. The key to each of these groups is that it is made up of people who have known each other since childhood. When Rip Hamilton made it big in the NBA, his group of friends from his neighborhood made it big with him. When Dale Jr. is at home taking a break from NASCAR, he is usually with his group of childhood friends. LeBron James is a little different; his friends actually form a management group that handles much of his business ventures.

While they may differ somewhat, one thing is true: for the friends of these celebrities, being a follower has its benefits. Life as LeBron's business manager is probably better than working a regular nine to five job, right?

Read Matthew 16:24-26. Jesus had a lot to say about being a follower. He did not promise fame. He did not promise fortune. He did not promise comfort. But look at what He did promise: "For whoever wants to save his life will lose it, but whoever loses his life for me will find it."

There are two truths in this Scripture passage worth mentioning. First, Jesus absolutely, positively commands that we follow Him. There is no other way around it. Christ does not desire your lukewarm commitment. He expects 100 percent of your devotion. Second, He expects your devotion knowing full well the cost of following Him. Jesus knows your road will be tough. He knows following Him is not easy. So, why does He still command us to be His disciples?

The answer is easy: Jesus knows that following Him leads to life . . . Life free from the penalty of sin . . . Life free from the power of death. Jesus longs for you to follow after Him, and to lead others to do the same.

While it might not have the same privileges of this world, following Jesus does have its benefits. So . . . what are you waiting for?

Am I A Follower?

Jesus told His disciples that He would suffer greatly for them, and for the world.

He was saying to them that there was a great cost to living the life He was called to live.

Jesus teaches us that God's call on our lives means giving up our own agendas. It means taking on His life, the life He commands us to live in the Bible.

This particular unit in this book is going to challenge you to examine yourself a bit. <u>TAKE THIS SERIOUSLY!</u> It's an awesome opportunity for God to work in your life. So, if you're ready to go a little deeper, think about the following:

What if an outsider, a stranger, someone you didn't know looked at your attitude, your actions, and your lifestyle—all the things that make you who you are? If this person looked at all of these things, how would he or she describe you? Write down your thoughts.

Still, the bigger question is, "Would someone watching how you live your life recognize it as the life of someone who truly follows Jesus?" Circle yes, no, or maybe below.

Yes   No   Maybe

You have the chance now to go deeper in your relationship with Christ. If you are not following Him like you wish you were, now is the day to do something about it.

Here's a start: Make a list of people whom you think do an awesome job of living their lives as a follower of Christ. Seriously, write their names down.

Now, follow through by talking to these people. Ask them when they decided to truly follow Christ. Ask them what following Christ has cost them. Ask them what they have learned about God and about themselves as a result.

Finally, pray right now that God would give you a heart to follow Him. Ask for the strength to turn toward Him and to live a life worthy of a disciple of Christ.

A LIST OF THE CALLED

You are one in a long list of people God has called to follow Him. Remember the people?

God called . . .

ABRAM

The LORD had said to Abram, "Leave your country, your people and your father's household and go to the land I will show you." —Genesis 12:1

MOSES

When the LORD saw that he had gone over to look, God called to him from within the bush, "Moses! Moses!" And Moses said, "Here I am." —Exodus 3:4

SAMUEL

Then the LORD called Samuel. Samuel answered, "Here I am." —1 Samuel 3:4

DAVID

So Samuel took the horn of oil and anointed him in the presence of his brothers, and from that day on the Spirit of the LORD came upon David in power. —1 Samuel 16:13

JONAH

The word of the LORD came to Jonah son of Amittai: "Go to the great city of Nineveh and preach against it, because its wickedness has come up before me." —Jonah 1:1-2

ISAIAH

Then I heard the voice of the Lord saying, "Whom shall I send? And who will go for us?" And I said, "Here am I. Send me!" —Isaiah 6:8

THE DISCIPLES

Jesus called them, and immediately they left the boat and their father and followed him. —Matthew 4:21-22

PAUL

"Who are you, Lord?" Saul asked. "I am Jesus, whom you are persecuting," he replied. —Acts 9:5

YOU...

"Here I am! I stand at the door and knock. If anyone hears my voice and opens the door, I will come in and eat with him, and he with me." —Revelation 3:20

What Does It Mean to Follow?

Part 1

In Matthew chapter 16 Jesus gave a definition of what it looks like to follow Him:

Then Jesus said to his disciples, "If anyone would come after me, he must deny himself and take up his cross and follow me. For whoever wants to save his life will lose it, but whoever loses his life for me will find it. What good will it be for a man if he gains the whole world, yet forfeits his soul? Or what can a man give in exchange for his soul? —Matthew 16:24-26

Wow. . . Quite a vivid picture of what it means to follow after Jesus. There are really three steps involved in being a disciple of Christ. Can you spot them? Denying yourself, taking up your cross, and, of course, following Christ.

Circle these three steps in the verse above.

Let's take a minute to look at what it means to deny yourself. You'll get a chance to go deeper into the meaning of the other two steps later on in this chapter.

What do you think it means to deny yourself? Got any ideas?

It's pretty straightforward, actually. It simply means you must put Jesus and His plans for the world before your plans for your own life. It's asking the question, "How can I live my life in a way that glorifies God and points people to Him?"

The cool thing about the Greek word Matthew used in this verse is that it implies an ongoing practice of following. Jesus knew it wouldn't be easy. You may have to wake up every day and say, "Jesus, today I give you my will." But Jesus expects nothing less from you.

What changes do you need to make in your life to put your will aside and live like Jesus called you to live?

Do you put some things in your life before your relationship with Jesus? If so, list them in the space below.

Write a prayer to God asking Him to help you submit your will to Him. Thank Him for loving you enough to provide a way for you to be in relationship with Him.

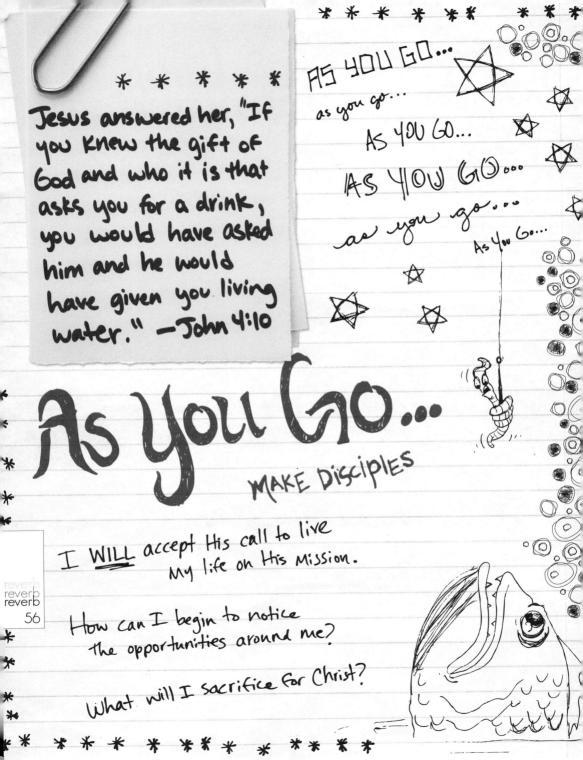

Jesus answered her, "If you knew the gift of God and who it is that asks you for a drink, you would have asked him and he would have given you living water." —John 4:10

AS YOU GO...
as you go...
AS YOU GO...
AS YOU GO...
as you go...
As You Go...

As You Go...

MAKE DISCIPLES

I **WILL** accept His call to live my life on His mission.

How can I begin to notice the opportunities around me?

What will I sacrifice for Christ?

Devotion

Opportunity.

Think about that word for a second or two. What meanings come to mind? Maybe it means something kind of like good luck, or good fortune. Like, "Jenny's car broke down, giving me the opportunity to be the hero and offer her a ride home." Or maybe it brings to mind the positive possibilities of the future . . . as in, "Going to college increases the potential for a meaningful job opportunity."

The truth is that both of these meanings are important—especially when it comes to living out God's call to be on mission with Him. Opportunity to make a difference is all around you. And living on mission for God provides you with ample opportunity for impacting the world.

But there is one important thing about opportunity worth mentioning: An opportunity must either be seized or missed. To seize an opportunity is to realize the potential of the moment. To not seize an opportunity is to miss it. Any potential is then lost.

Keep this idea in mind as you read John 4:1-26. That sounds like a lot of Scripture to read, but it flows quickly. Why? Because this passage is an amazing retelling of an encounter Jesus had with a woman. But not just any woman. This woman was a Samaritan, and Jesus was a Jew. Why does that matter? Well, Samaritans and Jews literally hated one another. That is one reason Jesus' conversation was so shocking to this woman. The other reason was because during the course of their conversation, the woman figured out that Jesus was the Son of God. Which, you know, is a pretty shocking thing to realize.

Jesus' conversation with the Samaritan woman led to many in her town coming to a saving faith in Jesus Christ. This couldn't have happened if Jesus had not seized the opportunity to have a meaningful, life-on-life interaction with this woman.

Jesus commanded His followers to live life on His mission. But He did more than that. He followed it up with His actions. Jesus practiced what He preached.

Do you seize opportunities to impact the world in Christ's name? Or do you let them pass by you? What will it take for you to become more committed to using your life to make a difference for Jesus? Pray to God today, asking Him to give you the strength to make the best of the opportunities He puts in your path.

I would be so COOL to travel across Europe. on a bike... on a bus... on a train... Yes a train!

How cool! ☺

traveling on a train is doing life as you go. eating in the dining car... sleeping in a bunk. talking to people. thinking. All the while, you're moving! As your headed to any where you're going, you're living out your life

what do they look like? what are they reading?

meeting people. where are they from? where are they going?

what are they listening to? what do they believe in?

POST CARD

Place Postage Here

Domestic Island Possessions
Canada
Cuba

Our spiritual journey is a lot like traveling on a train.
Jesus is our map. The journey is living our life as His followers.
We are headed somewhere, right? An Awesome destination.
A perfect reunion with the Maker. BUT, life doesn't wait
for the destination. We are living life every day as we
journey closer to our eternal home. On this journey,
we encounter others. Do we get to know them?
Do we find out where they are headed?
    where they have been? Do we ever invite them
to travel along with us? To join us on our journey

I want my time on the journey to make a difference.
I want to live for CHRIST as I travel towards my destination.

IF YOU'RE TAKING THIS BOOK SERIOUSLY, you're about ten pages into a section that is all about your response to God's call.

Don't be confused. The call being discussed isn't the call to salvation. You're not being asked to "get saved." Correct or not, the assumption is if you're this far into this book, you're probably a person who considers him or herself a Christ-follower.

No, the response you're being challenged with is different than a profession of faith.

The response you're being challenged with is all about how you choose to live your life. You see, you have been given an amazing gift. Life. And you better fully realize that it is a gift. It is a gift that was given to you based on nothing you brought to the table. And it is a gift that can disappear in the blink of an eye.

You are only guaranteed this moment. Anything after this is gravy.

Knowing the fleeting nature of your time on this earth, knowing who it was that authored your life, knowing Jesus' call to be on mission for Him, knowing the chance you have been given to make a major impact on this world for Jesus, knowing all of these things . . .

What do you say?

Christ has called you. His mission is moving forward. It is not waiting on you. In fact, if you haven't responded you're missing it.

But it's not too late.

Will you respond to Christ's call? Will you say "yes," to being on mission with Him? Will you agree to give your days to Him to be used for His purposes?

If you choose, write a prayer of response to God telling Him you will follow Him, giving your life to make a difference for Him in this world.

What hesitations do you have about answering the call?

If you are not absolutely living your life for Christ, giving yourself to be on His mission of love for the world, what does that say about your belief in His message?

It Starts Now * * * * * *

Do you ever get the sense that when people talk about you and your life that they are talking about something far, far away? It seems like oftentimes when adults talk to teenagers about their lives, it's as if "life" is something that doesn't start until after you're a teenager. Think about it . . .

Middle school prepares you for high school.

High school prepares you for college.

College prepares you for your job.

When you get a job you're ready to get married.

When you get married you can start thinking about having kids.

Once you've had kids, then of course, you're ready to start living life. While no adult would openly tell you this is the case, it's implied isn't it? Too often teenagers like you are subtly told that the life you are now living is somehow preparation for life ahead.

Nothing could be further from the truth.

You have been created and called by God. He wants you (yes, you) to be a crucial part in His plans.

God doesn't want you to start tomorrow . . . or next year . . . or once you're in college . . . or once you're married.

He wants you to live for Him today. Right now.

Would I recognize Jesus' voice if He called me?

Am I always immediate in my response to Jesus?
Do I hesitate?
I want to be immediate!
I want to go **AT ONCE.**

As Jesus was walking beside the Sea of Galilee, he saw two brothers, Simon called Peter and his brother Andrew. They were casting a net into the lake, for they were fisherman. "Come, follow me," Jesus said, "and I will make you fishers of men." At once they left their nets and followed him.
— Matthew 4:18-20

The disciples left AT ONCE.
They didn't even kiss their mom goodbye.

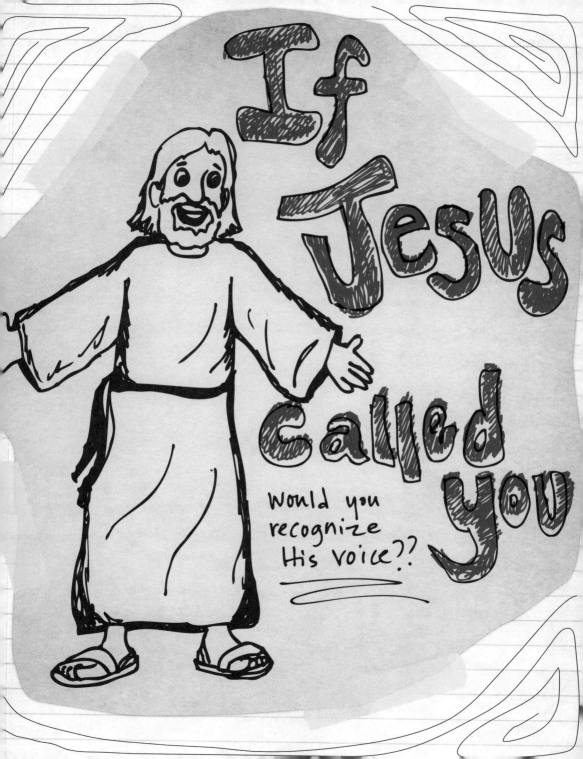

THE STORY OF PAUL

He even went to other cities to get Christians.

ARGH!

Until one day...

Paul instantly knew that Jesus was talking to him. Paul figured out he had been wrong all along.

LORD, is that you?

Paul was blinded and could not see.

Paul went on to write more of the New Testament than any other writer. 13 books in all.

Paul would go on to be the greatest influencer of Christianity other than Christ Himself. All because he answered the call!

"Everyone who calls on the name of the Lord will be saved." How, then, can they **CALL** on the one they have not believed in? And how can they believe in the one of whom they have not heard? And how can they hear without **SOMEONE PREACHING TO THEM?** And how can they preach unless **THEY ARE SENT?** As it is written, "How beautiful are the feet of those who bring good news!" —Romans 10:13–15

God, help me have the beautiful feet of one who brings the world the good news of YOU

What Does it Mean to Follow?
Part 2

Remember back a few pages when you studied Jesus' definition of discipleship in Matthew 16:24-26? Let's take another look:

Then Jesus said to his disciples, "If anyone would come after me, he must (deny himself) and take up his cross and follow me. For whoever wants to save his life will lose it, but whoever loses his life for me will find it. What good will it be for a man if he gains the whole world, yet forfeits his soul? Or what can a man give in exchange for his soul? —Matthew 16:24-26

If you recall, these activities give you the chance to define the three different components of what Jesus said makes up a disciple. In part one of this activity you learned exactly what it meant to "deny yourself." Take a moment and circle that phrase in the verse above.

Now, you're about to learn the meaning of the second step in discipleship, taking up your cross. Underline the phrase "take up his cross" in the passage above.

Do you have any guesses as to what this might mean? Write any thoughts in the space below.

When Jesus said a disciple must "take up his cross," He was using the image of crucifixion to speak about discipleship, which is pretty astounding. Keep in mind that crucifixion was a form of death the Romans used on the worst kind of criminals. It was an extremely shameful way to die, which is why it's striking that Jesus would use this picture as an image of what it means to follow Him. But if you think about it, it makes perfect sense. . . .

See, Jesus knows that following Him invites the world to turn against you. If you are living a life on mission for God, you will be ridiculed, shamed, and left out. But it's all a part of following after Christ. The world treated Him the exact same way.

Have you ever felt shamed or left out because you are a Christ-follower? Describe how that made you feel.

If you have not ever been left out or made fun of for your faith, have you considered that you might not be living the kind of life Jesus has called you to live? Being left out is no fun. But the cool thing is that you serve a King who experienced shame and ridicule. Jesus knows how you feel.

And, in the end, the reward for His followers is worth every bit of shame and tribulation.

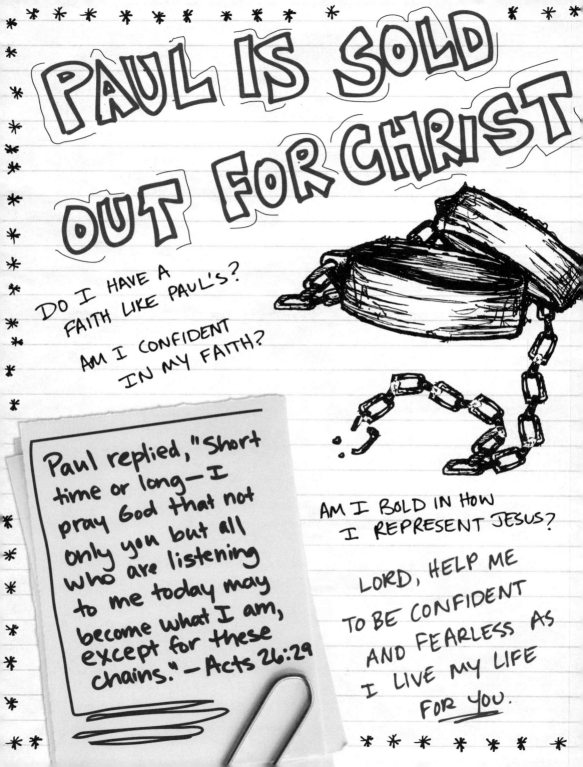

GOD EXPECTS YOU TO BE BOLD IN HOW YOU REPRESENT HIM TO THE WORLD. HE DOES NOT EXPECT YOU TO BE TIMID.

Why does God expect so much from you? After all, doesn't He know how hard it is to make a stand for Him in your world?

"I am the good shepherd; I know my sheep and my sheep know me" John 10:14

Jesus, the Son, and God, the Father, know their sheep. If you are a follower, then God knows you.

"And those he predestined, he also called" Romans 8:30

Not only does God know you, He has called you, personally, to follow Him.

"If anyone would come after me, he must deny himself and take up his cross and follow me" Mark 8:34

God expects you to follow Him in the right manner, submitting your life to Him, to be used for His glory.

"Therefore, as God's chosen people holy and dearly loved, clothe yourselves with compassion, kindness, humility, gentleness and patience" Colossians 3:12

God also expects you to live in a way that honors Him and demonstrates His characteristics to the world.

"Therefore, since we have such a hope, we are very bold" 2 Corinthians 3:12

Not only does God expect you to honor Him with your actions, He calls you to be a bold, courageous presence in your world.

"I am not ashamed of the gospel, because it is the power of God for the salvation of everyone who believes" Romans 1:16

God expects you to never back down from sharing the truth of the Gospel, through your words and your actions.

"For our light and momentary troubles are achieving for us an eternal glory that far outweighs them all" 2 Corinthians 4:17

See, Jesus does expect a lot. But it is because He knows you, loves you, has called you, and has given you the power to boldly live your life on His mission.

And if you do live your life for Him if won't be easy. But the reward that is waiting for you far outweighs anything this life has to offer.

reverb reverb reverb 69

devotion

Think for a moment about the brakes on your car. It's probably the first time you've thought about them in a while . . . maybe ever. And that's exactly the point. Your brakes are pretty important. They are not just important to the function of your car, but to your life. After all, when you go flying down the Interstate, at some point you'll need to stop. And unless you want that stop to be the result of a horrific crash, brakes come in handy.

Whether you think about it or not, you place your life's security in the brakes of your car over and over again. You probably don't think of that when you apply pressure on the left pedal. You simply trust that they'll work. Because of this, you have the confidence to drive at very high rates of speed.

Keep this example in your head as you read Acts 25:23–Acts 26:32. (Yeah, it seems like a lot to read, but it's a really cool story.) This story is one of the last chapters in the record we have of Paul's life. Paul had been arrested and was being taken before various Roman officials as part of his trial process. In this passage, Paul is speaking in front of King Agrippa and his sister Bernice.

Think back to what you just read in Acts. Think about the way Paul conducted himself. Isn't it amazing how boldly he stood up to Agrippa? Paul didn't miss a beat. He preached to this powerful King as if he were just another guy. How could Paul be so courageous in that situation?

As Christ-followers, when we know the certainty of God's call on our lives, our responses to God become automatic. We don't think, we react. This certainty allows us to move with God, acting and speaking as He leads us. In the same way you don't often think about the brakes in your car, our response to God should be just as automatic.

When we see a stop sign, we press the brakes and stop. Every time. Often without thinking. When we see an opportunity to make a difference for Christ, we should respond immediately. Every time. God expects us to join Him any time there is a need. Do you live like Paul? Are you fearless? Do you respond when the opportunity arises?

Therefore, since we have such a hope, we are very **bold**.
—2 Corinthians 3:12

be strong & courageous.

Do not be afraid or terrified because of them, for the LORD your God goes with you; he will never leave you nor forsake you.—Deuteronomy 31:6

Though an army besiege me, my heart **will not fear**.—Psalm 27:3

For the LORD will be your confidence and will keep your foot from being snared.
—Proverbs 3:26

Wait for the LORD; **be strong** and take heart and wait for the LORD.— Psalm 27:14

So **do not fear**, for I am with you; do not be dismayed, for I am your God. I will strengthen you and help you; I will uphold you with my righteous right hand.—Isaiah 41:10

Such confidence as this is ours through Christ before God.—2 Corinthians 3:4

The LORD is with me; **i will not be afraid**. What can man do to me?—Psalm 118:6

That is why, for Christ's sake, I delight in weaknesses, in insults, in hardships, in persecutions, in difficulties. For when I am weak, then **i am strong**.
—2 Corinthians 12:10

Finally, **be strong in the Lord** and in his mighty power.
—Ephesians 6:10

Do not let your hearts be troubled and **do not be afraid**.—John 14:28

God has called you to be in mission with Him. How are you responding?

Below is a long list of things you can do to be on mission with God.
Take a minute to read through them. Then, check the boxes for the activities
that you can complete to respond to God and live on mission with Him.

- ☐ Go to work
- ☐ Take a test
- ☐ Volunteer at your church
- ☐ Walk the dog
- ☐ Become an astronaut
- ☐ Volunteer at a homeless shelter
- ☐ Take out your neighbor's trash
- ☐ Go to the mall
- ☐ Mow the lawn
- ☐ Sit down
- ☐ Catch fire-flies
- ☐ Eat breakfast
- ☐ Play basketball
- ☐ Stay at home
- ☐ Rake your neighbor's yard
- ☐ Play videogames
- ☐ Paint your neighbor's house
- ☐ Go to church
- ☐ Decorate a Christmas tree
- ☐ Get up
- ☐ Drink a drink
- ☐ Milk a cow
- ☐ Play baseball
- ☐ Eat a hamburger
- ☐ Bring a friend to church

- ☐ Jump rope
- ☐ Use a telescope
- ☐ Give money to the poor
- ☐ Paint your face
- ☐ Be kind to a stranger
- ☐ Eat supper
- ☐ Go to school
- ☐ Organize a community service project
- ☐ Play volleyball
- ☐ Pray for the poor
- ☐ Listen to a praise song
- ☐ Dance in the rain
- ☐ Be kind to someone who is different
- ☐ Give money to your church
- ☐ Do palates
- ☐ Make waffles
- ☐ Read your bible
- ☐ Take a cab
- ☐ Fast for a day
- ☐ Give up TV for a week
- ☐ Go for a jog
- ☐ Adopt a pet
- ☐ Talk to a stranger
- ☐ Take a bus

- ☐ Give something up
- ☐ Work out
- ☐ Sing a song
- ☐ Be kind to an enemy
- ☐ Listen to music
- ☐ Volunteer at a foodbank
- ☐ Ride a rollercoaster
- ☐ Eat jellybeans
- ☐ Go on a mission trip
- ☐ Read a book
- ☐ Go to the library
- ☐ Listen to a friend
- ☐ Make a cake
- ☐ Give someone clothes
- ☐ Take a picture
- ☐ Play an instrument
- ☐ Draw a picture
- ☐ Write on a friend's Facebook wall
- ☐ Share coffee with a stranger
- ☐ Fly a kite
- ☐ Pray for the outcast
- ☐ Text your friend
- ☐ Post a picture on Facebook
- ☐ Brush your dog's teeth

- ☐ Watch a movie
- ☐ Write a play
- ☐ Make a movie
- ☐ Make coffee
- ☐ Write a book
- ☐ Drink coffee
- ☐ Give someone food
- ☐ Share your faith with someone
- ☐ Pray for someone
- ☐ Text your sister
- ☐ Clean a neighbor's house
- ☐ Ride a horse
- ☐ Walk your dog
- ☐ Rollerskate
- ☐ Swim in the lake
- ☐ Visit the sick
- ☐ Blow up a balloon
- ☐ Swat a fly
- ☐ Pray for the sick
- ☐ Trim your cat's toenails
- ☐ Bake cookies
- ☐ Drive to school
- ☐ Give to the poor
- ☐ Go to class
- ☐ Study for a test
- ☐ Play tennis

DO YOU BELIEVE IN JESUS? Would you consider yourself a Christ-follower?

Because you're reading this, you probably answered "yes" to the above questions.

So let's assume you believe in Jesus and that you are serious about following Him. If that's a safe assumption, it's probably also safe to assume that your life is decidedly different from the lives of those around you. After all, as a follower of Christ you're identified with Him in your actions and words . . . right? It's probably also safe to assume that you never miss an opportunity to talk about the difference Christ has made in your life. And that you never miss the chance to boldly defend God and His plan for the world. Right?

If you find yourself thinking that your life doesn't exactly match up with that last paragraph, you're not alone. Too often, we let opportunities to speak about Christ pass us by. Too often we hesitate to obey God's call on our lives.

Why do you think Christ-followers sometimes hesitate to take a stand for Him? What are the obstacles that stand in their way?

How does living boldly for Christ show those around you that you are 100% sure of God and His call on your life?

What does being timid about Christ say to the world about whether or not you really believe God and the promises He has made through Scripture?

God has called you to be a part of His mission. If you accept His call and live your life accordingly, you are saying to God that you believe Him and His promises. If you constantly turn away from God's call, you are communicating to Him and to others that God is not trustworthy. You are saying that you do not trust His promises.

Don't be fearful or timid. Be certain of your faith. Be sure of God's Word. Live your life boldly on mission for Him.

The word of The Lord came to Jonah son of Amittai: "Go to the great city of Ninevah and preach against it, because its wickedness has come up before me." But Jonah ran away from the Lord and headed for Tarshish. —Jonah 1:1-3

Yikes! Jonah really blew it. I'd hate to be him!

Am I more like Jonah than I'd like to admit? Haven't I disobeyed God's call before?

hesitancy

disobedience

JONAH = RUN FROM GOD = ON A BOAT IN A STORM = SWALLOWED BY A FISH = PUKED UP ON A BEACH

Run Away!!!

HERE'S ANOTHER QUESTION FOR YOU:

Do you think God knows best for your life?

You might be quick to say, "yes, of course." But what do your actions say? What does your attitude say? If your life doesn't demonstrate your belief that God knows best, you might need to reevaluate what is truly important to you.

When have you ever felt God leading you to do something? What was it?

How did you respond?

Have you ever disobeyed or ignored God when He has called you to do something? How did that work out for you?

Here's a secret for you: God will call you to be a part of His plan. When He does, your task is to obey. When you do obey, God chooses to bless you by allowing you to fulfill your role as a part of His plan to reach the world. However, when you disobey God, you are depriving yourself of His amazing blessing.

Do you want to be in the center of God's will for your life? Then it's easy . . . Simply obey Him next time you feel His leading. You might just be surprised what He will use you to accomplish.

FOUND THIS LETTER TODAY...

Lauren,

Where do I even start? I have so much I need to say...

I'll start with **I'M SORRY**. You were right all along.

I should have gone with you the first time. But it took me being apart from you to realize how much I need you. I don't want to live ~~without the~~ without you in my life.

So... what I'm saying is that I'm coming. I want to be with you.

If it's not too late...

Love Always,
   Me

WOW ... I wonder what he did wrong?
Sounds like maybe he blew it.

I wonder where she went?
Paris? India? Texas????

COULD I EVER
LOVE SOMEONE
ENOUGH TO FOLLOW
THEM ANYWHERE?

WHO R UR NINEVITES?

When we read the story of Jonah, we find out a pretty ugly truth about him: Jonah didn't really like the Ninevites. Actually, we don't really know whether or not he liked them. What we do know is that he didn't care about them. He wanted God to destroy them because they were evil. Jonah actually got angry at God because God had compassion on the people of Ninevah.

Before you judge, you need to think about one thing. Answer one question. Who are your Ninevites? Who are the people that, if you were honest, you simply don't like.

Homosexuals?   Is it the Goth kids?   Is it white people?

Black kids?

Is it the Jocks at your school?   The Poor?   Hispanics?

If you're honest enough (and brave enough), write in the space below the people that it is hard for you to love.

Even if your reasons don't make sense, confess to God what it is about those people that make them so hard for you to love.

Now, if you are sincere, if you really mean it, take a moment and pray the following prayer to God: Lord, I believe that you are a God of grace, mercy, and compassion. I believe that no one is beyond your love. After all, you love me and I have sin in my heart. I am guilty of being unloving to those you love. Help me to learn to have compassion on those people whom I find it hard to be compassionate towards.

Now, challenge yourself to pray this prayer until your heart truly is softened toward your Ninevites.

DEVOTION

When people ask you to do something, your response says a great deal about your relationship with them. Do you say, "yes" and agree to what is asked? Or do you say, "no"? It depends, right? If it's your mom or dad asking you to take out the trash, you will more than likely say, "yes." The reasons for this can range from respect to fear of punishment. But even fear of punishment says something about your relationship. You know your mom or dad is going to follow through with any threat of punishment. Again, your response depends on your relationship.

Read Jonah 1:1-4; 3:1-6; 4:1-3. This is not the whole story of Jonah. It is a record of his responses to God. You know the story of Jonah. God called Jonah to minister to Ninevah. What happened next isn't pretty. Jonah fled. Storm rolls in. Jonah goes overboard. Fish swallows. Fish throws up. Jonah heads to Ninevah. Jonah would inevitably do the work God wanted him to. But not after experiencing some harsh consequences. And not without a bad attitude.

Think about Jonah's responses. Is it true that something about his response speaks to his relationship with God? That would seem to be the case. See, Jonah put his needs first. This says that Jonah valued his own insecurities and fears more than he valued his service for God. While Jonah eventually got it right, he still managed to get it wrong in the end through selfish thinking.

God is constantly calling you . . . through His word, through His creation, through His Spirit, and through others. How are you responding to His call? How does a positive response communicate your love for Him? How does a negative response affect your usability for God's work?

Challenge yourself to commit to a positive, immediate response to God's call on your life. How can you be making a difference for Christ today?

* * * * *

Then I heard the voice of the Lord saying, "Whom shall I send? And who will go for us?" And I said, "Here am I. Send me!"
— Isaiah 6:8

WHOA... Isaiah saw GOD!

God, help me to be like Isaiah. Help ~~my~~ me want to go where you need me.

* OBEDIENCE   * SAYING YES TO GOD   * MESSENGER

Seraphs -R- Awesome

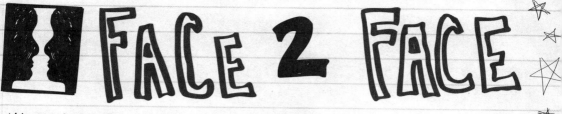# FACE 2 FACE

HAVE YOU EVER COME FACE TO FACE WITH GOD?

Not in a literal sense . . . Have you ever been confronted by God and what He expects of you? If so, the first thing you probably became aware of was how unworthy you were to even have God consider you.

A long time ago, a guy named Isaiah had a similar idea go through his mind.

Take a second and read Isaiah 6:1-8. Isaiah was at the Temple worshipping or offering a sacrifice when God appeared to him. The first thing Isaiah realized was how sinful he was.

Isaiah's response is the right one. When faced with God's perfection and greatness, we suddenly realize how worthless we are.

When was the last time you were truly aware of your sin in the presence of God? In your own words, write how you felt when faced with God's greatness.

What do you say to God when you are convicted of your sin? Or, a better question, are you convicted of your sin? If not, why not?

Here's a harsh truth: You cannot be all you can be for the Lord unless you deal with any habitual sin in your life. What is standing in the way of you serving God?

Why do you continue to let it stand in the way? Are you ready to give this over to God? Don't delay. Make the decision to give it up right now.

The ♥ of God

By now you have a pretty good idea of God's heart and desire for the world. You know that God has a deep love for the nations. You know that He has set a plan in motion to draw all people to Him. You know He has chosen you to be a part of that plan. But to be a part of God's plan, you have to be committed to having a heart like God. What does that mean anyway?

Let's look at a few things we know about God. Then, on the next page you will get a chance to grade yourself on how well you exemplify God's qualities. It's an awesome chance for you to get to evaluate your spiritual life and to know which areas to ask God to help you grow.

LET'S GET STARTED

God Loves All People
For God so loved the world that he gave his one and only Son, that whoever believes in him shall not perish but have eternal life. —John 3:16

God is Forgiving
If we confess our sins, he is faithful and just and will forgive us our sins and purify us from all unrighteousness. —1 John 1:9

God Has Mercy on the Poor and the Outcasts
Sing to the LORD! Give praise to the LORD! He rescues the life of the needy from the hands of the wicked. —Jeremiah 20:13

God is Giving
The lions may grow weak and hungry, but those who seek the LORD lack no good thing. —Psalm 34:10

God Sees People's Needs
The eyes of all look to you, and you give them their food at the proper time. —Psalm 145:15

God is Compassionate
Because of the LORD'S great love we are not consumed, for his compassions never fail. —Lamentation 3:22

God is Patient
The Lord is not slow in keeping his promise, as some understand slowness. He is patient with you, not wanting anyone to perish, but everyone to come to repentance. —2 Peter 3:9

I LOVE ALL PEOPLE

1   5   10

I AM FORGIVING

1   5   10

I HAVE MERCY ON THE POOR AND THE OUTCASTS

1   5   10

I AM GIVING

1   5   10

I SEE PEOPLE'S NEEDS

1   5   10

I AM COMPASSIONATE

1   5   10

I AM PATIENT

1   5   10

When you're finished, ask yourself the following questions:

Which areas are you strong in?

Which areas are you weak in?

How can you use your strengths to make a difference for God in the world?

How can you work to make you weaknesses strengths?

What Does It Mean to Follow? Part 3

In the first two parts of this activity you've already learned what it means to deny yourself and to take up your cross. In this last part you will look at what it means to follow Christ.

As a reminder, here is another look at Matthew 16:24:

THEN JESUS SAID TO HIS DISCIPLES, "IF ANYONE WOULD COME AFTER ME, HE MUST DENY HIMSELF AND TAKE UP HIS CROSS AND FOLLOW ME.

As a review, in your own words write what it means to deny yourself.

Do the same for the phrase "take up your cross." What does that mean to you?

Now let's focus on this word "follow." What does it mean to follow Jesus? The Greek word used for "follow" was a word that Matthew was very fond of. The word as it pertains to discipleship appears more in Matthew than any other Gospel. While the word follow can be used to describe following anyone or anything, it is used in Matthew's Gospel as a special word describing discipleship. All you have to do is look at how Jesus used the word. Here are a few samples:

"COME, FOLLOW ME," JESUS SAID, "AND I WILL MAKE YOU FISHERS OF MEN." AT ONCE THEY LEFT THEIR NETS AND FOLLOWED HIM.—MATTHEW 4:19-20

BUT JESUS TOLD HIM, "FOLLOW ME, AND LET THE DEAD BURY THEIR OWN DEAD."—MATTHEW 8:22

ANYONE WHO DOES NOT TAKE HIS CROSS AND FOLLOW ME IS NOT WORTHY OF ME.—MATTHEW 10:38

JESUS ANSWERED, "IF YOU WANT TO BE PERFECT, GO, SELL YOUR POSSESSIONS AND GIVE TO THE POOR, AND YOU WILL HAVE TREASURE IN HEAVEN. THEN COME, FOLLOW ME."—MATTHEW 19:21

Who do you follow? Do you follow Christ? Or do you follow someone else? Do you follow your selfish desires? Do you follow the crowd? Do you follow a boyfriend or girlfriend? Do you follow what's trendy?

Answer this question: If someone who didn't know you were to examine your life and look at the decisions you make and the priorities you have, who or what would they say you follow?

If you are following someone or something other than Jesus, what changes do you need to make to begin following Christ?

Write a prayer telling Jesus you want to follow Him. Confess to Him that you may not have always followed Him like you should. Ask the Spirit to empower you with the strength to turn from those things that are in your way.

The difference between JONAH and ISAIAH

The difference between Jonah and Isaiah is the difference between a delayed response and an immediate response. It's the difference between obedience and disobedience. Here's a quick comparison:

JONAH

WHAT WAS GOD'S CALL?

"Go to the great city of Nineveh and preach against it, because its wickedness has come up before me" (Jon 1:2)

WHAT WAS JONAH AND ISAIAH'S RESPONSE?

"But Jonah ran away from the Lord and headed for Tarshish" (Jon 1:3)

WHAT WAS THE RESULT OF JONAH AND ISAIAH'S RESPONSE?

Jonah boarded a ship. God sent a storm. Jonah was thrown overboard to stop the storm. A fish swallowed Jonah. Jonah was in the fish's belly for three days. Finally made it to Ninevah.

WHAT WAS JONAH AND ISAIAH'S ATTITUDE WHEN ENCOUNTERING GOD?

Jonah was selfish and self-centered; kept a bad attitude even as he was doing God's will (Jon 4:1-11).

ISAIAH

Then I heard the voice of the Lord saying, "Whom shall I send? And who will go for us?" (Is. 6:8)

"And [Isaiah] said, "Here am I. Send me!" (Is. 6:8)

Isaiah became one of the greatest prophets in Israel's history; prophesied under three different kings; prophesied the destruction of Israel, but also the coming Messiah.

"Woe to me!" [Isaiah] cried. "I am ruined! For I am a man of unclean lips, and I live among a people of unclean lips, and my eyes have seen the King, the Lord Almighty" (Is. 6:5).

the answer

IN THE CULTURE SURROUNDING YOU, THE VERY IDEA OF LOVE HAS BEEN TWISTED AND CORRUPTED. WHERE DO YOU GO TO FIND TRUE, PERFECT LOVE? THE BIBLE IS A GREAT STARTING POINT. AFTER ALL, IT'S IMPOSSIBLE TO READ THE GOSPELS AND NOT ENCOUNTER JESUS' ALL ENCOMPASSING MESSAGE OF LOVE. BUT THE LOVE OF CHRIST IN GOD ISN'T FOUND SOLELY IN THE GOSPELS. IT'S A THREAD THAT COURSES THROUGHOUT SCRIPTURE, WEAVING ITS WAY FROM GENESIS TO REVELATION. OVER THE NEXT SIX SESSIONS, YOU WILL COME FACE-TO-FACE WITH THE MOST FOUNDATIONAL ELEMENT IN A CHRISTIAN'S LIFE, NAMELY, **GOD'S LOVE.**

session 1 THE SOURCE—Pg 88-93

session 2 LOVE'S GREAT SACRIFICE—Pg 94-99

session 3 ANSWERING LOVE—Pg 100-105

session 4 VERTICAL WORSHIP—Pg 106-111

session 5 VERTICAL OBEDIENCE—Pg 112-117

session 6 HORIZONTAL LIVING—Pg 118-123

All you need is love, love.
Love is all you need.

ALL YOU NEED IS LOVE. LOVE. LOVE.
LOVE IS ALL YOU NEED.
—ALL YOU NEED IS LOVE, LENNON/MCCARTNEY

DEVOTION

Think for a moment about a glass of water. If you had to identify the most essential property of water, what would it be? You would probably say, "The essential property of water is its wetness."

Think about fire. What would you say was its essential property? While you might list a few different things, fire's essential property would have to be "heat."

Sugar is sweet. Ice is cold. Water is wet. Fire is hot. And God . . . Well, God is **LOVE**.

Read 1 John 4:7-8. John knew a thing or two about **LOVE**. John was one of Jesus' closest companions. Along with Peter and James, John was in the "inner circle" of disciples, a group that Jesus went to great lengths to teach and mentor. John was there at nearly every important episode in Jesus' life. John understood Jesus and His message of love and redemption. So when John says "God is **LOVE**," we ought to pay attention.

There are a lot of things we could say about God. He has so many wonderful attributes that make Him worthy of our praise, **LOVE**, and devotion. He is perfectly wise, powerful, good, just, forgiving, merciful, holy, compassionate . . . the list goes on. If you think of God and His attributes as an ever-flowing, eternal river that runs throughout time and history, the source of that river must surely be His **LOVE**.

If you know God, you know **LOVE**.
God is the source of all **LOVE**.

DO NOT SEEK REVENGE OR BEAR A GRUDGE AGAINST ONE OF YOUR PEOPLE, BUT **LOVE** YOUR NEIGHBOR AS YOURSELF. I AM THE LORD. **LEVITICUS 19:18** LOVE T LORD YOUR GOD WITH ALL YOUR HEART AND WITH ALL YOUR SOUL AND WITH AL YOUR STRENGTH. **DEUTERONOMY 6:5** KNOW THEREFORE THAT THE LORD YOUR GOD IS GOD; HE IS THE FAITHFUL GOD, KEEPING HIS COVENANT OF **LOVE** TO A THOUSAND GENERATIONS OF THOSE WHO **LOVE** HIM AND KEEP HIS COMMANDS. **DEUTERONOMY 7:9** GIVE THANKS TO THE LORD, FOR HE IS GOOD; HIS **LOVE** ENDURES FOREVER. **1 CHRONICLES 16:34** TURN, O LORD, AND DELIVER ME: SA ME BECAUSE OF YOUR UNFAILING **LOVE**. **PSALM 6:4** SURELY GOODNESS AND **LOVE** WILL FOLLOW ME ALL THE DAYS OF MY LIFE, AND I WILL DWELL IN THE HOUSE OF THE LORD FOREVER. **PSALM 23:6** FOR YOUR **LOVE** IS EVER BEFORE ME, AND I WALK CONTINUALLY IN YOUR TRUTH. **PSALM 26:3** YOUR **LOVE**, O LOR REACHES TO THE HEAVENS, YOUR FAITHFULNESS TO THE SKIES. **PSALM 36:5** F AS HIGH AS THE HEAVENS ARE ABOVE THE EARTH, SO GREAT IS HIS **LOVE** FOR THOSE WHO FEAR HIM. **PSALM 103:11** BECAUSE OF THE LORD'S GREAT **LOVE** W ARE NOT CONSUMED, FOR HIS COMPASSIONS NEVER FAIL. **LAMENTATIONS 3:22** HE ANSWERED: "**LOVE** THE LORD YOUR GOD WITH ALL YOUR HEART AND WITH ALL YOUR SOUL AND WITH ALL YOUR STRENGTH AND WITH ALL YOUR MIND'; AND, '**LOVE** YOUR NEIGHBOR AS YOURSELF.'" **LUKE 10:27** IF YOU **LOVE** ME, YOU WILL OBEY WHAT I COMMAND. **JOHN 14:15** MY COMMAND IS THIS: **LOVE** EACH OTHER AS I HAVE **LOVED** YOU. **JOHN 15:12** BUT GOD DEMONSTRATES HIS OWN **LOVE** FOR US IN THIS: WHILE WE WERE STILL SINNERS, CHRIST DIED FOR US. **ROMANS 5:8** WHO SHALL SEPARATE US FROM THE **LOVE** OF CHRIST? **ROMANS 8:35** MAY THE GRACE OF THE LORD JESUS CHRIST, AND THE **LOVE** OF GOD, AND THE FELLOWSHIP OF THE HOLY SPIRIT BE WITH YOU ALL. **2 CORINTHIANS 13:14** MAY THE LORD DIRECT YOUR HEARTS INTO GOD'S **LOVE** AND CHRIST'S PERSEVERANCE. **2 THESSALONIANS 3:5** FOR GOD DID NOT GIVE US A SPIRIT OF TIMIDITY, BUT A SPIRIT OF POWER, OF **LOVE** AND OF SELF-DISCIPLINE. **2 TIMOTHY 1:7** ABOVE ALL, **LOVE** EACH OTHER DEEPLY, BECAUSE **LOVE** COVERS OVER A MULTITUDE OF SINS. **1 PETER 4:8** THIS IS HOW WE KNOW WHAT **LOVE** IS: JESUS CHRIST LAID DOWN HIS LIFE FOR US, AND WE OUGHT TO LAY DOWN OUR LIVES FOR OUR BROTHERS. **1 JOHN 3:16** WHOEVER DOES NOT **LOVE** DOES NOT KNOW GOD, BECAUSE GOD IS **LOVE**. **1 JOHN 4:8** KEEP YOURSELVES IN GOD'S **LOVE** AS YOU WAIT FOR THE MERCY OF OUR LORD JESUS CHRIST TO BRING YOU TO ETERNAL LIFE. **JUDE 21**

God is LOVE

reverb
reverb
reverb
91

Wish you were here!

What's up?

I bet you're pretty busy these days. I won't write too much, but I did want to make sure I said "thanks" for all the help. I don't know if I would have made it without your help. I mean it. But then, I guess you know that, right?

Anyway, just wanted to touch base with you.

Thanks again!

Chris

POST CARD

J
P.O. Box 1240
Boston, MA 02215-3406

DEVOTION

Do you remember the conversation with your parents about your desire to be born? "Mom, Dad . . . I have prepared a presentation outlining all the motivating factors for my birth. As you'll notice on the pie chart on the next slide, while there will be lots of dirty diapers on the front end, once I am old enough to cut the grass the savings on landscaping alone will make up for it."

Do you remember this conversation? Of course not . . . because it never happened. You had no input whatsoever in the decision to be born. You exist because your mom and your dad decided they wanted you.

Read Genesis 1:26-31. In this passage, you pick up the story of God creating the world. Before the world there was only God. Out of nothing, He literally spoke the world into existence. And once he had finished creating the world, He chose to place man and woman in the middle of it. God didn't have to make humans. Adam and Eve certainly had no say in it. So, why did God make us?

The answer is found in Genesis 1:28. After God had made Adam and Eve, he blessed them. Then, look what happened next . . . "He said to them." Did you see it? It happened pretty quickly. Look again. God made man and woman, then he spoke to them! How amazing is that? God did not speak to the trees or plants. He spoke to humans. He made people for relationship. God made us out of His great **LOVE**.

You don't deserve to be here. And you don't deserve God's **LOVE**. (Don't feel badly... No one does.) But amazingly, He chose for you to be in His world. And God most definitely **LOVES** you. In fact, it was His **LOVE** for you that motivated your existence. Think about that. His **LOVE** is the source of your life. Have you thanked

This is how much God loved the world.

THIS IS HOW MUCH GOD LOVED THE WORLD: HE GAVE HIS SON, HIS ONE AND ONLY SON. AND THIS IS WHY: SO THAT NO ONE NEED BE DESTROYED: BY BELIEVING IN HIM, ANYONE CAN HAVE A WHOLE AND LASTING LIFE.
—JESUS, JOHN 3:16 (THE MESSAGE)

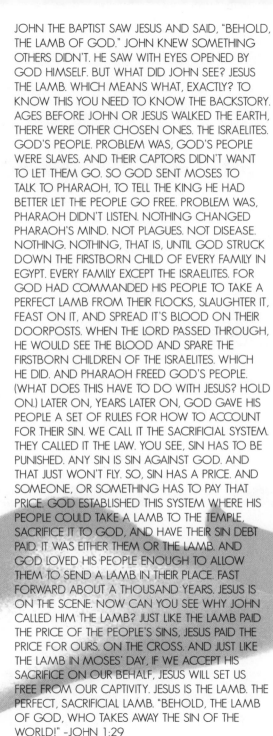

JOHN THE BAPTIST SAW JESUS AND SAID, "BEHOLD, THE LAMB OF GOD." JOHN KNEW SOMETHING OTHERS DIDN'T. HE SAW WITH EYES OPENED BY GOD HIMSELF. BUT WHAT DID JOHN SEE? JESUS THE LAMB. WHICH MEANS WHAT, EXACTLY? TO KNOW THIS YOU NEED TO KNOW THE BACKSTORY. AGES BEFORE JOHN OR JESUS WALKED THE EARTH, THERE WERE OTHER CHOSEN ONES. THE ISRAELITES. GOD'S PEOPLE. PROBLEM WAS, GOD'S PEOPLE WERE SLAVES. AND THEIR CAPTORS DIDN'T WANT TO LET THEM GO. SO GOD SENT MOSES TO TALK TO PHARAOH, TO TELL THE KING HE HAD BETTER LET THE PEOPLE GO FREE. PROBLEM WAS, PHARAOH DIDN'T LISTEN. NOTHING CHANGED PHARAOH'S MIND. NOT PLAGUES. NOT DISEASE. NOTHING. NOTHING, THAT IS, UNTIL GOD STRUCK DOWN THE FIRSTBORN CHILD OF EVERY FAMILY IN EGYPT. EVERY FAMILY EXCEPT THE ISRAELITES. FOR GOD HAD COMMANDED HIS PEOPLE TO TAKE A PERFECT LAMB FROM THEIR FLOCKS, SLAUGHTER IT, FEAST ON IT, AND SPREAD IT'S BLOOD ON THEIR DOORPOSTS. WHEN THE LORD PASSED THROUGH, HE WOULD SEE THE BLOOD AND SPARE THE FIRSTBORN CHILDREN OF THE ISRAELITES. WHICH HE DID. AND PHARAOH FREED GOD'S PEOPLE. (WHAT DOES THIS HAVE TO DO WITH JESUS? HOLD ON.) LATER ON, YEARS LATER ON, GOD GAVE HIS PEOPLE A SET OF RULES FOR HOW TO ACCOUNT FOR THEIR SIN. WE CALL IT THE SACRIFICIAL SYSTEM. THEY CALLED IT THE LAW. YOU SEE, SIN HAS TO BE PUNISHED. ANY SIN IS SIN AGAINST GOD. AND THAT JUST WON'T FLY. SO, SIN HAS A PRICE. AND SOMEONE, OR SOMETHING HAS TO PAY THAT PRICE. GOD ESTABLISHED THIS SYSTEM WHERE HIS PEOPLE COULD TAKE A LAMB TO THE TEMPLE, SACRIFICE IT TO GOD, AND HAVE THEIR SIN DEBT PAID. IT WAS EITHER THEM OR THE LAMB. AND GOD LOVED HIS PEOPLE ENOUGH TO ALLOW THEM TO SEND A LAMB IN THEIR PLACE. FAST FORWARD ABOUT A THOUSAND YEARS. JESUS IS ON THE SCENE. NOW CAN YOU SEE WHY JOHN CALLED HIM THE LAMB? JUST LIKE THE LAMB PAID THE PRICE OF THE PEOPLE'S SINS, JESUS PAID THE PRICE FOR OURS. ON THE CROSS. AND JUST LIKE THE LAMB IN MOSES' DAY, IF WE ACCEPT HIS SACRIFICE ON OUR BEHALF, JESUS WILL SET US FREE FROM OUR CAPTIVITY. JESUS IS THE LAMB. THE PERFECT, SACRIFICIAL LAMB. "BEHOLD, THE LAMB OF GOD, WHO TAKES AWAY THE SIN OF THE WORLD!" -JOHN 1:29

LIVING
SACRIFICE

When you read the word, **SACRIFICE**, what words or images come to mind?

Where in the world around you do see examples of sacrifice?

List some practical ways or things you could sacrifice for the good of those around you.

Take a moment to say a prayer that God would reveal to you the needs of those around you, and ways you might can meet them . . . even if it means giving up something of your own.

LONDON

POST CARD

Dear Chris,

It's so good to hear from you. I love it when you write. Don't worry about "writing too much." I always have time for you!

Thank you for your appreciation, but as you know, I am always here to help. I understand how you were feeling and was so glad to see you pull through.

Before I let you go I wanted to tell you how proud I am of you. I have enjoyed watching you these last few months. You're really growing up . . .

Love Always,

J

ps Good luck with your test next week!

Chris Reynolds
2183 Wynn Dr.
San Diego, CA 92101

U.S.
42

Happily Ever After

DEVOTION

How far would you go to demonstrate your **LOVE** for someone? If your first thought was, "Depends on who we're talking about," then you're probably like most people. After all, you **LOVE** people differently, don't you? Think of your distant cousin you only see once every few years. Your **LOVE** for him or her is different than your **LOVE** for, say, your mom, right? The lengths you would go to show your **LOVE** for your mom are probably a lot greater than the lengths you would go to show your **LOVE** for your cousin. You'd give up a kidney for mom. For cousin whatsherface? Uh . . . . not so much.

Read 1 John 4:9-10. We're back with our good friend John the Apostle. As we mentioned in last session's devotion, John knew Jesus as intimately as anyone. He was one of Jesus' most trusted disciples. In fact, John was known as "the beloved disciple." As much as anyone, John grasped the significance of Jesus' identity and His mission. John knew that God sent Jesus to this world. John knew Jesus was God's most precious gift to His creation.

Why was Jesus such a precious gift? Because Jesus was God's answer to the question of how we as humans could once-and-for-all pay our sin-debt. You see, God is perfectly good. Any sin is a sin against Him and His standards. God is also perfectly just. And all sin must be punished. If God didn't punish all sin, He wouldn't be worth our devotion. God sent Jesus to pay the debt for our sins, clearing the way for us to have eternal fellowship with God.

How far would you go to demonstrate your **LOVE** for someone? Not as far as God did to demonstrate His **LOVE** for you. God sent His only Son to die for you. And Jesus willingly obeyed. Why? Because God **LOVES** you. Jesus **LOVES** you. Even when you are unlovable. **That is AMAZING LOVE!**

Jesus is LOVE

But love your enemies, do good to them; BUT LOVE YOUR ENEMIES, DO GOOD TO THEM, AND LEND TO THEM WITHOUT EXPECTING TO GET ANYTHING BACK.

– JESUS, LUKE 6:35

live love diary

If you think about it, everything you do in life, can be done in love.

Ask yourself the question, "How did I demonstrate love today in my actions?"

Take this journal with you today and record times you lived out your love for others. Or open it again tonight and recap your day.

Be as detailed as you can.

Howdy! Me again ... Sorry I
haven't written in a while. You
know me! Always kind of crazy ...

Well, I don't have much to write
about. But I saw the coolest
thing today and you crossed my
mind. It's dumb, I know... But I
was driving and I looked up and
out of nowhere this rainbow was
stretching across the whole sky. I
actually pulled over to look at it!
Can you believe that? Anyway, I
thought about you and how I miss
you. I wish we could be closer.
But I understand, you know?

OK. Better run. I'll write sooner
next time. Promise!

Chris

POST CARD

J.
P.O. Box 12940
Boston, MA 02215-3496

LOVING GOD LOVING PEOPLE

The Books of Matthew, Mark, and Luke all tell a similar story. In each of these books, Jesus is in the company of some of the Jewish religious leaders.

In Matthew and Mark's account, Jesus was asked by one of the Jewish religious leaders what the greatest commandment of the Law was. This guy was trying to trick Jesus, but Jesus turned it around on him.

Jesus actually answered in an amazing way. If He had answered incorrectly, or had given an answer that wasn't well thought out, the Jewish leaders could have accused Him of trying to abolish parts of the Law.

A lot was riding on Jesus' answer.

BEFORE YOU GO ON, STOP FOR A MINUTE AND READ DEUTERONOMY 6:5 AND LEVITICUS 19:18.

Sum up Deuteronomy 6:5 in one sentence.

Sum up Leviticus 19:18 in one sentence.

We might not get it now, some 2,000 years later, but at the time what Jesus did by putting these two commandments together was a big, big deal.

In answering the Jewish leaders this way, Jesus combined the emphasis of the first half of the Ten Commandments (obligation to God) with the second half (obligation to others). But Jesus did more than that . . .

LOOK BACK AT MATTHEW 22. COMPARE VERSE 37 WITH VERSE 39. CIRCLE THE POWERFUL WORD THAT APPEARS IN BOTH VERSES. DID YOU CATCH IT? YOU SHOULD HAVE CIRCLED THE WORD **LOVE**.

The most amazing thing Jesus did was make His answer all about love. It wasn't about rule following. It wasn't about stale religion. Jesus said we must love God, and love people.

LOVE GOD. LOVE PEOPLE.

It really is that simple.

Think about any changes you might need to make in your life to begin to show more love and thankfulness to God. Think about any attitudes or issues you have that get in the way of loving others. Now, pray to God that He will help you put into practice the changes you need to make in your life.

We **LOVE**

God

We are shaped and fashioned...
WE ARE SHAPED AND FASHIONED
BY WHAT WE LOVE.
—JOHANN WOLFGANG VON GOETHE

sail away

Dear Chris,

Chris . . . you make me smile! I loved that you thought of me when you saw that rainbow. They are beautiful, aren't they? Sometimes the colors are so bright you'd swear they were painted right on the clouds. I've always been fond of them myself . . .

I know at times it feels like we are far apart. I know that can be tough. But remember that our love keeps us close even though distance separates us. I am always with you in that way . . . And these letters help, don't they? I love to hear from you . . . even when you don't have anything important to say!

Love Always,
J

p.s. If you see Tyson, please tell him I am thinking about him and that I miss him.

POST CARD

Chris Reynolds
2183 Wynn Dr.
San Diego, CA 92101

This page is for you. Express your love to God through words or pictures.

DEVOTION

ACTIONS. REACTIONS.

Webster's defines the word action as "a thing done." An action can be anything, right? Standing up, throwing a paper airplane, or texting a friend are all actions. It's pretty simple, really. Anything you do can be considered an action.

On the other hand, a reaction is defined as "a response to some treatment, situation, or stimulus." Basically, a reaction is a response to any action. Want some examples? Think about the actions we listed above. If you were to suddenly stand up in the middle of a nice dinner with your boyfriend or girlfriend, he or she might react with confusion. (Or they might look at you like you've lost it.) If you were to throw a paper airplane in the hallway and hit your principle in the eye, his or her reaction would probably spell trouble for you. And if you were texting your friend to tell her that your crush just asked you to the homecoming dance, her reaction would be excitement.

The nature of the reaction depends on the nature of the action.

Read Psalm 103:1-12. This is one of the many psalms written by David. You know David. The guy that killed the giant. The one who had to hide out from King Saul while Saul tried to kill him. The one who was said to have a "heart like God's." David was an awesome king, undoubtedly the best ruler Israel ever had. He wasn't perfect. (You might remember the whole Bathsheba incident.) But he **LOVED** the Lord. And many of his psalms reflect this **LOVE**.

If you go back and look at this psalm one more time, you realize something pretty cool. This psalm is all about actions and reactions. David lists some of the amazing things God has done, not just for David, but for the nation of Israel. David says that God forgives sins, heals diseases, satisfies desires, works righteousness for the oppressed, gives freely of His compassion while patiently doling out His anger, and so on, and so on. These are some pretty awesome actions. But what is the reaction?

David makes it clear: His reaction to all of God's actions is to lift up praise and worship to God. The appropriate reaction to God's **LOVE** is **LOVE** in return. How cool is that?

You have to ask yourself this question: "How have I been responding to all the ways God has shown me love in my life?" If your answer is anything less than giving God the praise He is due, you might need to spend some time examining your heart.

God has done so much for you. His actions demonstrate His **LOVE**. Does your reaction demonstrate praise?

Respond to *LOVE*

PRAYER POSTURE

You've learned that worship is one of the ways you should respond to God's amazing love for you.

PRAISE IS A HUGE PART OF WORSHIP. AND PRAYER IS ONE OF THE MAIN WAYS WE PRAISE GOD.

Have you ever considered how you pray?
The Bible has a lot to say about the posture—or the position of your body—when you pray.

Have you ever thought about your posture when you pray? Here's a challenge: Spend some time in prayer praising God because of His love for you. But, this time, try some of the different postures listed below:

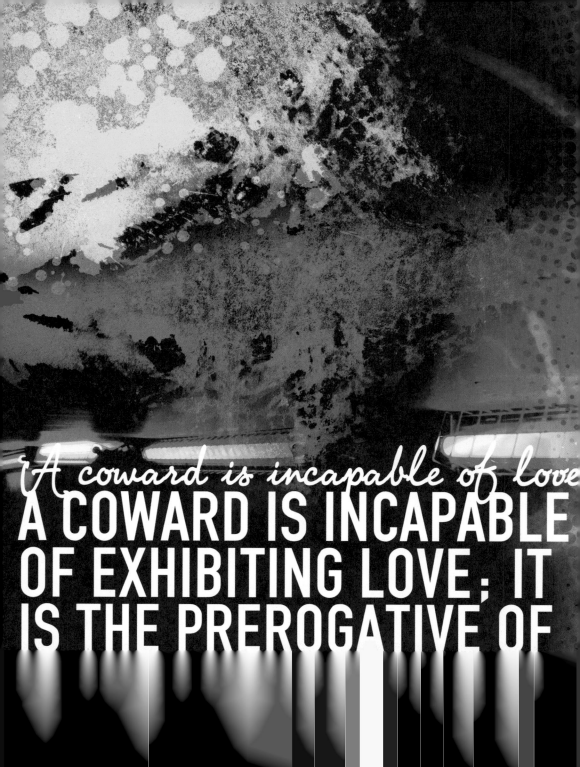

A coward is incapable of love

A COWARD IS INCAPABLE OF EXHIBITING LOVE; IT IS THE PREROGATIVE OF

CLIMB HIGHER

Chris,

My heart is breaking for you . . . It makes me so sad to see you hurting. I know how badly you wanted this. You had invested so much of yourself in it.

I know it might not make you feel better now, but know that everything happens for a reason. Even though you can't see the big picture, I am willing to bet that some good will come of this. Keep your head up! Don't lose hope. And know that more than anything, I am here when you need me. Don't hesitate to write.

Again, I am so sad you are hurting. I love you.

Love Always,

J

POST CARD

Chris Reynolds
2183 Wynn Dr.
San Diego, CA 92101

Follow His LOVE

DEVOTION

Read John 14:15-24.

Jesus' words are pretty straightforward, aren't they?

Those who say they love me show it by doing what I say. Those who say they **LOVE** me but don't do what I say don't really **LOVE** me.

How do these words make you feel? How are you tempted to respond? Do you feel like they are too harsh? After all, no one can obey Jesus all the time, right? You try, and for the most part you do pretty well. But, occasionally you slip up. Does this mean you don't **LOVE** Jesus? If this is the standard, does anyone really **LOVE** Jesus?

If you read this and think Jesus is harsh and maybe a little demanding, maybe that's not all that bad. Some of what Jesus had to say was a little harsh. See, we tend to turn Jesus into a wimp most of the time. We want Jesus to fix our problems and make us feel good when we feel bad. But most of the time we just want Him to stay out of our business. So, in this sense it's probably a good thing that Jesus rattles our cages a bit.

If this seems demanding, again, this is probably OK. Jesus does demand a great deal from us. He demands absolute loyalty and devotion. He expects to have no other competition for our affection. And here's the kicker: our obedience results from us being loyal and devoted to God. They go hand in hand.

Jesus doesn't ask for us to keep a list of do's and don'ts and to check them off one at a time. That's not obedience to Jesus. That's obedience to morality. Jesus expects us to give Him our hearts, and in turn to take up His heart. He wants us to live as He lived, to view the world as He did, to see people as His children. And to look at our lives as important pieces in His big-picture plan.

When we live this way, we are living obediently. And our obedience is a demonstration to God of just how much we **LOVE** Him.

I'm not sure how to start. First of all,
thanks for the kind words. I needed that! I
guess deep down I knew you were right. But
it still hurts, you know? Anyway, thanks for
always being there. I felt better after hearing from you.

I guess part of me still kind of wonders
why it didn't work out, you know? But I
do believe you. I have to believe there is
some bigger plan for me. You helped remind me
of that. And that helped me get through it...
more than you know.

So, before I go I feel like, maybe I need to
apologize. The reason I didn't write sooner
is because... well, because I was mad at you. I
know, I know. I had no reason to be. I was
just upset. Please forgive me and know that
I do really appreciate all you do for me.

Anyway... I hope you understand.

Love,

Chris

WHERE HISTORY COMES TO LIFE

thanks.
U.S
42

POST CARD

J
P.O. Box 12940
Boston, ma 02215-3496

DEVOTION

Picture this image in your mind: A sunny day, wispy white clouds float by on a blanket of rich blue. Cruising down the Interstate, top down, music playing, a teenage guy. Not a care in the world. **LOVING** life.

But suddenly he sees something that causes him to slow down. Up ahead a police officer is stopped in the road waving her arms, her car lights flashing. The guy puts on the brakes and as he comes to a stop, rolls down his window.

"Just wanted you to know the bridge is out up ahead," the officer kindly says.

"Whew! Thank you for telling me, officer," he replies. "Have a great day!" The young guy then proceeds to slam his foot down on the gas and peel off, barreling straight towards the collapsed bridge.

This story makes no sense, right? Why? Because if the guy were really given such instruction, he would pay attention; he would listen to the warnings and then obey them. In this type of scenario, everyone would heed the potentially lifesaving advice.

Why is it sometimes different with God's Word?

Read James 1:21-24. What is the first thing you see? Verse 21 says it takes humility to accept the Word of God. You see, humans struggle with thinking we know it all. But it is not enough to merely listen to the word and know what it says, is it?

Quite clearly verse 22 says that if you are only hearing God's Word and not putting it into action, you are fooling yourself. Like the guy speeding towards a broken bridge, full speed ahead, not doing what God teaches will only lead to disaster. You must hear God's Word and then let it impact every part of your life. These verses call you to live a life that reflects the teachings of the Bible.

What does your life reflect?

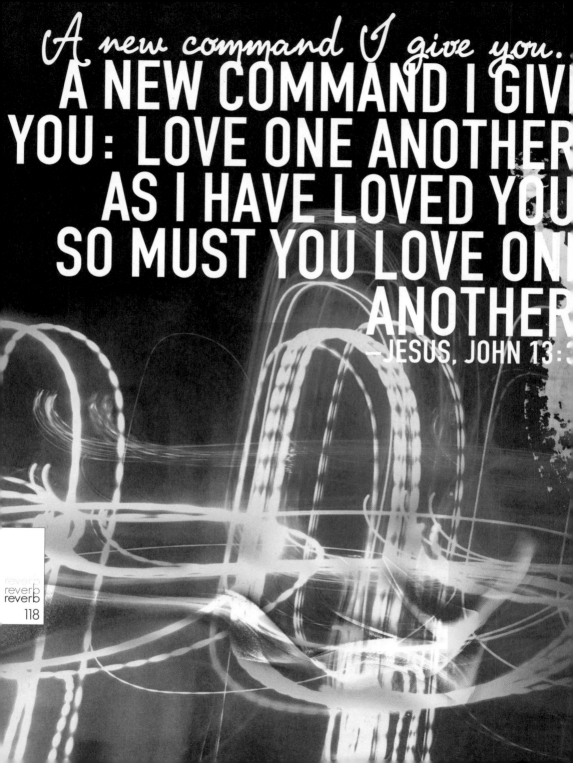

A new command I give you.

A NEW COMMAND I GIV
YOU: LOVE ONE ANOTHER
AS I HAVE LOVED YOU
SO MUST YOU LOVE ON
ANOTHER
—JESUS, JOHN 13:

WHO NEEDS LOVE?

When He was asked what the Greatest Commandment in the Law was, Jesus replied:

'LOVE THE LORD YOUR GOD WITH ALL YOUR HEART AND WITH ALL YOUR SOUL AND WITH ALL YOUR MIND.' THIS IS THE FIRST AND GREATEST COMMANDMENT.

AND THE SECOND IS LIKE IT: 'LOVE YOUR NEIGHBOR AS YOURSELF.' ALL THE LAW AND THE PROPHETS HANG ON THESE TWO COMMANDMENTS."

There are people in your life who need to see the love of Christ . . . through you. And they need it today.

e a moment and really think hard. Don't just pass over this. Who in your life needs love today?

te down their names:

Done, now take it one step further. Say their names out loud. I'm serious. Say their names out loud . . .

DO IT!!

have just spoken the names of people that you know need love today. If you don't
w love to them, who will?

at are you waiting on?

hello from the islands

Chris,

You make me laugh sometimes, you know that? First things first, as I have said before, I will always, always be here for you. Especially when you are hurting. So, while I appreciate your thanks, you don't have to be so surprised! I promise you I will never let you down. Ever . . .

Now, about you being mad at me . . . I do understand your frustration. Honestly, I do. And I know you were upset. But I need you to know that I am big enough to handle anything you bring my way. Next time you are angry or upset, don't give me the silent treatment . . . Write me immediately! I would much rather work through it with you than have you hurt anymore.

Remember, I love you . . . And there is nothing you can do to change that.

Love Always,

J

p.s. Next time you see Sara, please tell her I said thank you. She'll know what you mean . . .

U.S. 42

POST CARD

Chris Reynolds
2183 Wynn Dr.
San Diego, CA 92101

LOVE *Through Us*

HOW CAN I DEMONSTRATE LOVE TO OTHERS?

You could:

TAKE THEM TO DINNER

SHOOT THEM A TEXT JUST TO SAY HELLO

LISTEN TO THEM

FEED THEM

SIT WITH THEM AT THE DR.'S OFFICE

TAKE OUT THEIR TRASH

INVITE THEM TO YOUR HOUSE TO PLAY VIDEO GAMES

LEAVE A NOTE ON THEIR WALL

WASH THEIR CAR

BUY THEM ICE CREAM

GIVE UP SOMETHING FOR THEM

TAKE THEM TO A MOVIE

LEAVE A KIND COMMENT ON ONE OF THEIR PICTURES

VISIT THEM IN THE HOSPITAL

INVITE THEM TO HANG OUT WITH YOU AND YOUR FRIENDS

RAKE THEIR YARD

PAINT THEIR HOUSE

ASK IF THEY NEED HELP WITH ANYTHING

LET THEM KNOW YOU ARE PRAYING FOR THEM

BRING THEM TO CHURCH

TAKE THEM TO A BALLGAME

INVITE THEM TO SIT WITH YOU AT LUNCH

GIVE THEM YOUR TIME

SEND A TEXT TO SEE HOW THEIR DAY IS GOING

TALK TO THEM

BUY THEM A COAT

GIVE THEM YOUR AFFECTION

DO THEIR MAKEUP

OFFER THEM A RIDE HOME FROM SCHOOL

TAKE THEM TO A CONCERT

COOK THEM A MEAL

FIX THEIR ROOF

HELP THEM

THE SKY IS THE LIMIT

I got your last letter. Wow... you are so right. I should have come to you when I was upset.

It's funny. I've had a lot going on lately. I've been so busy. I've been confused about some stuff. But things are starting to make sense. And one of those things is our relationship. I finally get what you have been trying to tell me all along. You love me! You really love me. You love me for who I am today in spite of who I was yesterday or the day before.

I guess the more I understand this the more it changes things. It kind of makes my head hurt a little... But, I guess we have time to figure it all out, right? I can't wait...

Before I go I just wanted to say thank you.

And I love you.

Chris

POST CARD

J
P.O. Box 12940
Boston, MA 02215-3496

PICTURE THE SCENE: JESUS WAS IN HIS FINAL MOMENTS WITH HIS DISCIPLES BEFORE HE WOULD ASCEND FROM EARTH BACK TO HEAVEN. IN HIS LAST WORDS TO HIS CLOSEST FOLLOWERS, JESUS INSTRUCTED THE DISCIPLES TO GO THROUGHOUT THE WORLD AND MAKE DISCIPLES. HAVE YOU EVER WONDERED WHAT JESUS MEANT WHEN HE SAID "MAKE DISCIPLES"? THIS COMMAND IS ACTUALLY PRETTY IMPORTANT. IN FACT, IT'S AT THE HEART OF THE INDIVIDUAL CHRIST-FOLLOWER'S MISSION AND PURPOSE. ALL CHRIST-FOLLOWERS ARE CALLED TO BE A PART OF TEACHING OTHERS WHAT IT MEANS TO LIVE FOR JESUS. YOU ARE NO EXCEPTION.

DO YOU KNOW WHAT IT MEANS TO MAKE DISCIPLES OF YOUR FRIENDS? (DOES THE THOUGHT SCARE YOU?) BETTER YET, DO YOU EVEN FEEL AS IF YOU'RE EXPECTED TO DO SO? DO YOU FEEL EMPOWERED TO ACCEPT THE TASK OF DISCIPLING OTHERS? IF NOT, DON'T WORRY . . . YOU WILL AFTER YOU TAKE A JOURNEY THROUGH **TRANSFER**.

SESSION 1 TEACH *By* EXAMPLE — PG 126-131

SESSION 2 TESTIFY *to the* GOSPEL — PG 132-137

SESSION 3 TEACHING *What is* RIGHT — PG 138-143

SESSION 4 SERVE *the* WORLD/LOVE OTHERS — PG 144-149

SESSION 5 DO *Good* TO OTHERS — PG 150-155

SESSION 6 SHOW MERCY — PG 156-161

reverb
reverb
reverb

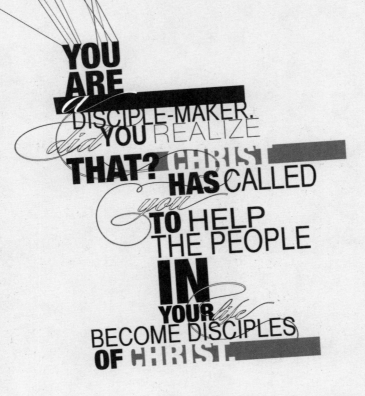

YOU ARE a DISCIPLE-MAKER. did YOU REALIZE THAT? CHRIST HAS CALLED you TO HELP THE PEOPLE IN YOUR life BECOME DISCIPLES OF CHRIST.

THE QUESTION IS, **"HOW DO YOU DO IT"**?

BEFORE YOU CAN HELP SOMEONE ELSE BECOME A DISCIPLE OF CHRIST, YOU HAVE TO KNOW WHAT BEING A DISCIPLE IS ALL ABOUT. YOU CAN'T KNOW THAT WITHOUT KNOWING GOD'S WORD. SO, KNOWING THE BIBLE IS THE FIRST STEP IN BECOMING A DISCIPLE-MAKER.

But it's not enough to know God's Word. You must share the truth of Scripture with the world. You can do that in two ways: talking about it and living your life according to it. Becoming a disciple-maker is a challenge. But with the help of the Holy Spirit, you can be an effective messenger for CHRIST.

DEVOTION

A BANDLEADER PLAYS A MEASURE OF MUSIC, DEMONSTRATING THE TIMING OF THE PIECE TO THE CLASS.

A TEACHER WORKS OUT AN ALGEBRA PROBLEM ON THE BOARD WHILE THE CLASS FOLLOWS ALONG.

A DAD TEACHES HIS TEENAGER THE INS-AND-OUTS OF CARPENTRY BY HELPING THE TEEN MEASURE, CUT, AND BUILD.

A COACH WALKS THE OFFENSE THROUGH THE PLAY SO HIS OR HER PLAYERS CAN SEE WHERE THEY NEED TO GO.

A MOM SHOWS HER TEENAGER HOW TO MAKE A SPECIAL DISH USING AN OLD FAMILY RECIPE.

What do these instances have in common? In each one someone is teaching some-one else by example. Teaching by example is highly effective. It allows the learner to see exactly what he or she needs to do to be successful.

Read 1 Timothy 4:11–16. First Timothy is a letter from Paul to Timothy. If you remember your Bible stories, Timothy was a young guy that Paul ran into while on one of his missionary journeys. Timothy had a lot of potential as a spiritual leader. Paul was the wise, experienced, grandfather-type who took Timothy under his wing and helped him grow spiritually. In many ways, Paul set the example for Timothy, modeling what it means to live life on mission. But in this passage, Paul turned the tables a little on Timothy.

Paul was nearing the end of his life, so he took the chance to impart some wisdom to Timothy. Paul, who had long set an example for Timothy, urged the young leader to now make sure that he set an example for his followers. Paul basically said, "Look, kid, it doesn't matter how young you are; people are watching. You are expected to show them the right way." The same can be said for you.

You are to live a life that sets an example for all who watch you. How do you accomplish this? First, you need to know what is expected of you. You need to know the standards. This can only happen if you read and apply the Bible. Next, you must make sure you are a vocal and active communicator of what you read in the Bible. Quite simply, you need to make sure you take the opportunity to talk about God's Word and to live it out.

You are called to be an example. You are called to be a disciple-maker. If you live and speak the truth of the Bible, God will do the rest. The Spirit will work through you to reach others for Christ. Which, if you think about it, is really pretty cool.

Step 1 IS TO...

SHOW

SHOW **THE** *world* THE IMPORTANCE **OF** CHRIST IN YOUR LIFE THROUGH *your* WORDS **AND** ACTIONS.

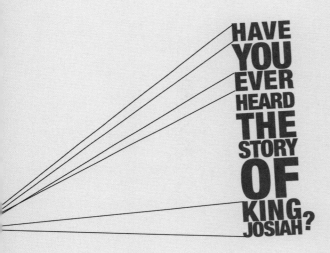

HAVE YOU EVER HEARD THE STORY OF KING JOSIAH?

Let's set the stage . . . King David is dead. His son, Solomon, is dead. And the Kingdom of Israel that had been so prosperous was now divided. Many of God's people had FORGOTTEN HIM. Kings ruled the northern Kingdom of Israel and the southern Kingdom of Judah. Some of these kings were good and reminded the people that God was still God. Others did evil and led the people astray.

Into this environment comes an EIGHT-YEAR-OLD KING NAMED JOSIAH. He was the King of Judah. He was a good person and he wanted to lead his people well. Part of being a good king was cleaning up the Temple. You see, the people had grown so far away from God that they had allowed THE LORD'S DWELLING PLACE to become run-down. As Josiah's men were cleaning out the Temple, something amazing happened.

Hilkiah, one of Josiah's main advisors, found the Book of the Law. Yep . . . that's right. Buried amid all the trash in the Temple was God's Word, the Scriptures that recorded all of the laws God had given Moses. When Josiah realized he and his people had not even been following God's Law, he GRIEVED AND MOURNED. But he didn't quit there. He gathered all of the people of Judah together and read everyone the Book of the Law. Then, he led the whole nation in recommitting to following God's Word.

Cool story, huh? But here's the kicker. . . Just like Josiah, you can be as good as you want. But YOU CAN'T FOLLOW WHAT YOU DON'T KNOW. In order to help others see the value in a relationship with Jesus, you have to live out God's Word. And before you can live out God's Word you have to know it.

DO YOU KNOW IT?

HIDING THE WORD IN YOUR HEART

In order to model the Word, you have to know it. You've heard this before, right? Have you ever wondered what is the best way to learn Scripture? There are a lot of ways to memorize God's Word. This page will list one way.

TRY FOLLOWING THESE STEPS TO MEMORIZE THIS VERSE OF SCRIPTURE. (IF YOU ALREADY HAVE MEMORIZED THIS SCRIPTURE, CHOOSE A DIFFERENT ONE AND FOLLOW THE STEPS.)

STEP 1
CHOOSE A VERSE

First, choose a verse to memorize. It's important to also read the verses surrounding it so you know exactly what's happening. For this activity, you will memorize 1 Timothy 4:12. Here's the verse: "Don't let anyone look down on you because you are young, but set an example for the believers in speech, in life, in love, in faith and in purity."—1 Timothy 4:12

STEP 2
READ THE VERSE SEVERAL TIMES

Now, read the verse several times. Read it very slowly. Think about the words. Try to see it in your head. Now, say it out loud a few times. Listen to yourself. Hear the words.

STEP 3
TRY TO SAY THE VERSE WITHOUT LOOKING

Chances are, you're not quite there yet. But give it a shot anyway.

STEP 4
WRITE THE VERSE

Start writing down the verse. You might have to look back at your Bible the first few times. The goal is to write the verse until you don't need to look at your Bible.

STEP 5
COME UP WITH A TRICK

This is where you can have some fun. Look at the verse you have (hopefully) memorized. Come up with some clues to help you re-member it. These clues might be images you see in your mind (F 1 Timothy 4:12 you might picture a baby to trigger the "young" pa of the verse.), letters you recall (For instance, to remember the phrase "in speech, in life, in love, in faith, and in purity" you migh picture the letters SLLFP in your mind.), or even the tune to your favorite song. The goal is to be able to trigger your memory whe you need to recall the verse.

HOPEFULLY THESE STEPS HELP. KNOWING SCRIPTURE IS KEY TO BEING A DISCIPLE-MAKER.

DO YOU WANT TO BE COUNTED WISE, TO BUILD A REPUTATION FOR WISDOM? HERE'S WHAT YOU DO: LIVE WELL, LIVE WISELY, LIVE HUMBLY. IT'S THE WAY YOU LIVE, NOT THE WAY YOU TALK, THAT COUNTS.

JAMES 3:13
(THE MESSAGE)

"DO NOT BE ASHAMED TO TALK ABOUT OUR LORD." Paul SAID THESE WORDS TO Timothy THOUSANDS OF YEARS AGO.

BUT THEY ARE STILL TRUE TODAY. ARE YOU EMBARRASSED TO TALK TO PEOPLE ABOUT JESUS?

Admit it. . . . there have been times when you wanted to talk with someone about God, but you got scared. Maybe you didn't want to offend that person. Maybe you were scared you wouldn't be able to answer his or her questions. Whatever the reason, you flaked out. You bailed. You kept quiet when you should have piped up.

As a Christ-follower you are called to never be ashamed to speak about Him. You are called to speak freely and powerfully about God to those who need to hear His truth.

Can you relate to this scenario? You're in a conversation with a friend or acquaintance. The conversation takes a turn, and suddenly you realize you have an amazing opportunity to talk about God. You have an opening! But before you can even formulate the words to say, you get all nervous. Your stomach churns. Your mind races. You struggle for the confidence to say anything, and before you know it the moment has passed. You kept quiet. And you missed a great opportunity to talk about the difference God has made in your life.

CAN YOU RELATE? IF YOU'RE LIKE MOST PEOPLE, YOU CAN.

THINK ABOUT SOME REAL-LIFE CHANCES YOU'VE HAD TO TALK WITH SOMEONE ABOUT CHRIST OR GOD, OR JUST BIG-PICTURE SPIRITUAL ISSUES . . . **BUT DIDN'T BECAUSE YOU GOT SCARED.**

List some reasons why you got nervous in that situation. Or if you want, just list some obstacles that teenagers in general experience while trying to share their faith.

IF YOU CAN REMEMBER A TIME WHEN YOU FLAKED OUT WHEN YOU HAD THE OPPORTUNITY TO SHARE YOUR FAITH, WHAT DID YOU FEEL LIKE AFTERWARDS?

WHY DO YOU THINK YOU FELT THIS WAY?

How should you have reacted? What could you have done differently to talk about your relationship with God?

Here's a thought: If you were lost in the desert with other people and you knew the pathway to an endless supply of water, would you share with the others or would you let them die of thirst?

IF GOD REALLY IS THE CREATOR OF THE UNIVERSE WHO SENT HIS SON TO DIE ON THE CROSS SO HUMANKIND WOULD NOT HAVE TO SPEND ETERNAL LIFE SEPARATED FROM HIM BECAUSE OF THEIR SINS . . . THEN WHY ARE WE SCARED TO TELL OTHERS?

You know the truth. Never be afraid to share it.

Step 1 IS TO...

SHOW

Step 2 IS TO...

SHARE

SHARE THE *story* OF GOD'S UNCONDITIONAL LOVE FOR THE WORLD AS *expressed* THROUGH HIS SON, JESUS.

FREE WRITING

This is a page where you will do what is called free-writing. In free-writing you receive a prompt—maybe an idea or a question—and then you begin writing. You don't pause, you don't think about what you are going to write before you write it . . . you just write. You write whatever comes to your mind when it comes to your mind.

So, here is your prompt: Think about the way you represent Jesus to the world. Do you represent Jesus boldly or do you run away from speaking boldly about Him?

Now DON'T hesitate... GET WRITING!

DEVOTION

WHAT DOES IT MEAN TO BE ASHAMED OF SOMETHING? IT MEANS TO BE HUMILIATED OR EMBARRASSED BY IT. BEING ASHAMED OF SOMETHING IS BEING FEARFUL IT MIGHT BRING YOU DOWN. WHEN YOU ARE ASHAMED OF SOMETHING, YOU TAKE ACTIONS TO DISASSOCIATE YOURSELF FROM IT OUT OF FEAR OF NEGATIVE CONSEQUENCES.

WHAT TYPES OF THINGS CAUSE A PERSON SHAME? A PERSON CAN BE ASHAMED OF SOMETHING HE OR SHE DID. LET'S SAY A TEENAGED GUY GETS ARRESTED FOR A DUI. THIS IS AN ACT THAT WOULD CAUSE THIS GUY TO FEEL ASHAMED AND EMBARRASSED. THE GUY WOULD RIGHTLY NOT WANT TO BE ASSOCIATED WITH HIS ARREST. HE WOULD LOGICALLY WANT TO DISTANCE HIMSELF FROM IT.

There are things that logically bring about feelings of shame and embarrassment. You can be ashamed of something you have done. You can be ashamed of something a family member has done. You can even be ashamed by the actions of a team, or a group of people, or a government, or some other element you might be involved in. Each of these specific entities can do things that would logically result in shame.

But you do not have an option when it comes to the things of God. You are not given a choice. You simply cannot live in such a way that you are ashamed of Christ, His story, or His presence in your life.

Read 2 Timothy 1:8–12. Paul says that even though the gospel had caused him to suffer, he would not stop talking about Jesus. Why? Because he is not ashamed of Christ.

Jesus has saved your life. He gave Himself willingly, allowing people to punish Him in the most gruesome ways imaginable. He took the shame of the crucifixion on Him because of your sins. He wasn't ashamed of you. Yet, as you remain silent when you know you should stand up for Christ, you tell the world you are ashamed of Him.

You have been given one life. That's it. You have one chance to make it count for Christ. You cannot do that by being embarrassed or ashamed of Jesus. You simply do not have that choice.

Don't be embarrassed. Be bold. Be courageous. Be strong. Be daring. Live for Christ!

LET'S TALK ABOUT GOD

what's

THE SECRET TO TALKING WITH PEOPLE ABOUT GOD? HOW ARE SOME PEOPLE SO GOOD AT IT WHEN YOU GET SO NERVOUS?

It's like they don't skip a beat. Maybe it's a friend or a parent or a relative or just someone you know from church. What is it about that person that makes him or her fearless?

WELL, KEEP READING . . .

There's a concept commonly practiced by people who are comfortable in talking with others about God. It's actually quite a simple approach. Here's the deal . . .

As you talk with people, think of simply talking about spiritual topics. What does that mean, you ask? It doesn't mean you have to come out of the gate preaching. What you need to start getting in the habit of doing is looking for openings to bring up spiritual matters. For example:

Sara: We had the coolest time at the beach. It was perfect.

Kayla: That's awesome. I love the beach. Sometimes I just stare at the water and wonder how all of it got there.

Did you see what Kayla did? She laid the foundation for a spiritual conversation. She's planted the seed to steer the conversation toward God as Creator. Let's look at another one:

Tyler: I just feel lost. I wanted this so badly. Now where am I going to go to college?

Chris: Listen, I know getting rejected is not cool. But have you ever thought that there might be some reason you didn't get accepted to that school? Like, maybe something good can come out of it?

Chris has opened the door to talk about God's sovereignty and His plan for His children.

See? You don't have to sound like some old-school, fire and brimstone preacher. Learning to look for an opportunity to steer a conversation toward spiritual things is a method many people use. Doing so makes the transition to talking about God almost natural.

Now, you still need to know what to say once you turn the conversation. But don't worry! The Holy Spirit is in you, helping you know what to say and when. So what are you waiting for? The next time you have a conversation with someone you know is not a Christ-follower, think about how you might lead that person to speak about spiritual things. You'll be amazed at how easy it is.

DO YOU DO WHAT IS RIGHT

DO YOU TRY NOT TO DO WHAT IS WRONG?

how DO YOU KNOW?

AFTER ALL, WHAT IS RIGHT *anyway?*

DOESN'T THE IDEA OF RIGHT & WRONG

DIFFER

WITH DIFFERENT PEOPLE?

Here's the deal: The world around you wants you to believe that the idea of right and wrong is open to interpretation, that it's relative. The problem with this line of thinking is that it runs exactly opposite to what God's Word teaches us about morality. The Bible teaches that God and His Word are the absolute standard for right and wrong. Rightness comes from God's character. Wrongness comes when we violate God's rules.

As a disciple-maker, you must help show people the truth about what is right and wrong. You can do this through telling them or through simply living in a right way. The goal is not that people would look at you and say how good you are, but that they would see your life and recognize that there is true goodness . . . and it starts with God.

DEVOTION

IMAGINE TURNING ON THE TV ONLY TO FIND THAT A MAJOR STORY WAS BREAKING. IT APPEARS THERE IS A PICTURE CIRCU- LATING ACROSS THE MEDIA THAT SHOWS PRESIDENT OBAMA AND OSAMA BIN LADEN PLAYING BASKETBALL TOGETHER. WHY WOULD THIS BE SUCH A BIG DEAL? BECAUSE SOME THINGS DO NOT, CANNOT, GO TOGETHER. THERE IS NO WAY THE PRESIDENT OF THE UNITED STATES WOULD BE HANGING OUT WITH A TER- RORIST. IT JUST WOULDN'T HAPPEN.

Presidents and terrorists don't mix. Neither do Red Sox and Yankee fans, oil and water, your mom and your Facebook profile, liberals and conservatives, cats and dogs . . . some things just are not meant to coexist.

LIKE *godliness* AND *ungodliness*

Read Titus 2:11–3:2. This passage is a letter from Paul to Titus. Ti- tus was one of Paul's closest friends. Titus served as Paul's special representative to the Corinthian church and was tasked with taking up a large contribution for the church in Jerusalem. Paul trusted Titus, who seemed to have some really good administrative skills and a confident personality. From this passage in the letter, we see Paul teaching Titus the importance of walking in a godly manner.

Paul used some pretty straightforward teaching. He basically said, "Say no to all of the stuff that is not of God. Say yes to all of the stuff that is of God." Seems simple enough. But then some questions come up. First of all, how do we know what is godly and what is not godly? And secondly, how do we have the power to say yes or no?

Paul answered these questions in a way that is pretty cool. The secret is found in verses 11–12. Paul said God's grace has been given to all, and that God's grace helps us know right from wrong. Paul also said God's grace teaches us to live the right way. It leads us to seek what is right and to turn from what is wrong. More importantly God promises to be with us on our journey. He promises to give us strength to do the right thing, day in and day out.

Godliness and ungodliness have no place with one another. Not in your life. Not in this world. Live in such a way that you say "no" to the things that lead you away from God and "yes" to things that build you up in God.

A letter...

Hey, there. How are you? I hope you're doing well. We don't know each other, so I guess we should start with an introduction. I'm the guy writing this book. Books don't just happen, you know. They have to be written. In this case, a few of my good friends and I got together and created this book for you. There were some things we wanted you to know, things we wish we knew when we were in high school. So . . . we made you this book.

Here's the deal. We're not a bunch of old folks. I'm the oldest guy and I am 32. Most of us are in our twenties. We're still on our journey, the same one you're on. We're still learning. We're still growing. We're still stumbling along. But we've learned some things along the way. And we think God wants us to tell you about them.

Thanks for listening to us. I hope you've enjoyed the book so far. Hopefully, we've earned your trust and managed to be faithful in the way we've talked to you about the things God has put on our hearts.

This letter deals with an issue that is important to us. As we were thinking about how to talk with you about it, we thought a letter might be the best way. A letter from us to you. Something personal. Between two friends. So, if it's not too much to ask, I'd love a few minutes of your time.

I want to talk to you about what it means to do right. To do good. To be good. I want to talk about what right is. And why it is important to do right things. And I think you might find what I have to say is different from what you might have heard before.

What is right, after all? Who decides? Your friends who aren't followers of Jesus might answer this question differently than you. They might say that right is whatever feels good. Or that there is no real standard for right. They might say what is right and wrong differs from person to person. I think you'd agree that this is probably the most common thing you hear in the world around you.

If you are a follower of Jesus, right and wrong is more clear cut for you. The Bible is God's Word to us. He inspired men to write it. And the Bible teaches you how to look at the world through the filter of God and His ways. The Bible teaches us what is right through God and His character. It teaches us what is right through Jesus' life and teachings. It teaches us what is right in the letters from guys like Paul, and Peter, and John.

The Bible is your source for right and wrong.

Even though it's that simple, there's still the question of how you put it into practice. What does the truth of the Bible mean for your life? What are you supposed to do with the knowledge of what is right and what is wrong?

Give me a couple more minutes to dig into the how and the why of doing right.

Quite simply, the Bible commands us to do what is right. Over and over again, Scripture calls us to do godly things and to not do ungodly things. And don't miss this: Jesus expects you to live rightly. To follow His example. He wants you to do right.

But the reason He wants you to do right might be different than you might expect. Jesus wants you to do right out of your love for Him. Out of your closeness to Him. He never desired or intended for people to live their lives according to some checklist, marking off all the good things they did and all the bad things they avoided. By yourself, doing good and being right won't earn you eternal life with God. Following Jesus will.

Following Jesus means turning away from the things of this world. That's a big, churchy sounding sentence, isn't it? But it's true. And if you begin to think about things in terms of what is godly and what is ungodly, you'll be surprised how clearly those distinctions will become. Even more surprising is what happens when you actually start living a life according to the right ways of God: people notice!

When you live your life according to the right things of God, people see the difference in you. The cool thing is, if you help them understand, they will grasp the fact that it's not you that makes you different, it's God. Your living will actually draw people to God.

Here's the secret we want you to know: you can't use right and wrong to beat people up. You can't use right and wrong to separate yourself from others. What do I mean? You can't look at those who do right as "us" and those who do wrong as "them." You must show people that living in God's "rightness" means freedom, life, hope, and love.

You can do it. The Holy Spirit promises to help guide you. And as you grow in your faith and understanding, God will continue to reveal to you His ways, and how they differ from the ways of the world.

I hope you've enjoyed the book so far. Stick with it. Finish strong. There is a lot more to learn and do.

good luck!

Godly

KINDNESS
PEACEFULNESS SERVANTHOOD
FOLLOWER
BOLDNESS
PURITY OF HEART HONESTY
UPLIFTING
COMPASSION ENCOURAGING KINDNESS
GENTLENESS
SACRIFICIAL LIVING GRACIOUSNESS
PURE WORDS
RIGHTEOUSNESS
HOLY LIVING SHOWING MERCY
SELF-CONROLLED
LOVE FOR ENEMIE
SELFLESS ATTITUDE CHRIST-LIKENESS
LOVE FOR THE LOST

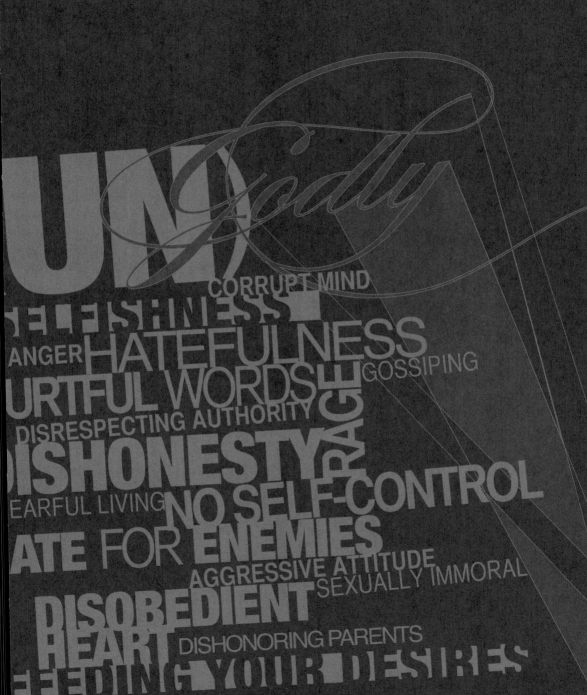

UNgodly

CORRUPT MIND

SELFISHNESS

ANGER HATEFULNESS

HURTFUL WORDS RAGE GOSSIPING

DISRESPECTING AUTHORITY

DISHONESTY

FEARFUL LIVING NO SELF-CONTROL

HATE FOR ENEMIES

AGGRESSIVE ATTITUDE

SEXUALLY IMMORAL

DISOBEDIENT

HEART DISHONORING PARENTS

FEEDING YOUR DESIRES

YOU CANNOT BE A DISCIPLE-MAKER *unless* YOU ARE MOTIVATED BY *love.* LOVE FOR OTHERS. AND NOT JUST ANY *love.* THE PERFECT, *unfailing* LOVE OF CHRIST. CHRIST'S LOVE IN YOU *motivates* YOUR LOVE FOR OTHERS.

Be honest . . . you'd rather take care of yourself than anyone else. You'd rather look after your own needs before you look after the needs of others. It's the sinful side of your human nature. But loving and following Christ changes that. When you love Christ, you begin to see others as people who need Jesus. And as a disciple-maker, your Christ-given love for others compels you to help lead them closer to Him.

LOVING CHRIST MEANS LOVING OTHERS.
LOVING OTHERS MEANS WANTING THEM
TO LOVE GOD. POINT OTHERS TO GOD BY
LOVING THEM AS CHRIST DOES.

HERE'S SOMETHING TO THINK ABOUT:

When you hear the word *service*, what comes to mind?

Do you think of acts of service? Chances are, this is where your mind goes first. When you hear the word service you probably think about cutting the grass for someone, or bringing meals to your shut-in neighbor, or going on a medical mission trip.

But there is another side of service. And that is an attitude of service. Acts of service are things you do. But you would not be inclined to do acts of service unless you had an attitude of service. It's an interesting twist, don't you think?

What makes an attitude of service? Well, read Philemon 4–6 to find out. Did you read it? Do you see the answer? Now, you're probably saying, I don't see anything in there about service. Well, in one way you might be right. Paul doesn't actually mention the word service in this passage. However, he says a great deal about the attitude of service.

Paul says that Philemon's love for all the saints is widely known. And it is Philemon's love that makes him a servant. Why? Because you can't do acts of service without an attitude of service. And you can't have an attitude of service unless you first love other people.

Loving others means putting them above yourself. It means looking at meeting their needs as more important than meeting your own. Loving others is a humbling act. And it is this valuing of others in love that motivates service. If you want to have an attitude of service, pray that God would lead you to love others more.

Once the love of God for others is in your heart, you will naturally want to live out an attitude and a lifestyle of serving. Your actions will speak to what is in your heart. And ultimately, God will be glorified because of it.

FREE WRITING

That's right . . . free-writing time again! This is another moment where you will be free-writing. Remember, in free-writing you receive a prompt, and then you begin writing. Don't pause, don't think about what you are going to write before you write it . . . just write. Write whatever comes to your mind when it comes to your mind.

Ready for your prompt? Here it is: As a disciple-maker you have to lead people to live the right way. How does that make you feel? Do you feel qualified? Is it a task you want to accept?

Now DON'T hesitate . . . GET WRITING!

Step **1** IS TO...

SHOW

Step **2** IS TO...

SHARE

Step **3** IS TO...

TEACH

THROUGH **YOUR** *words* **AND** ACTIONS, TEACH **THE** PEOPLE AROUND YOU **THE RIGHT** WAY TO LIVE, THE *godly* WAY TO LIVE.

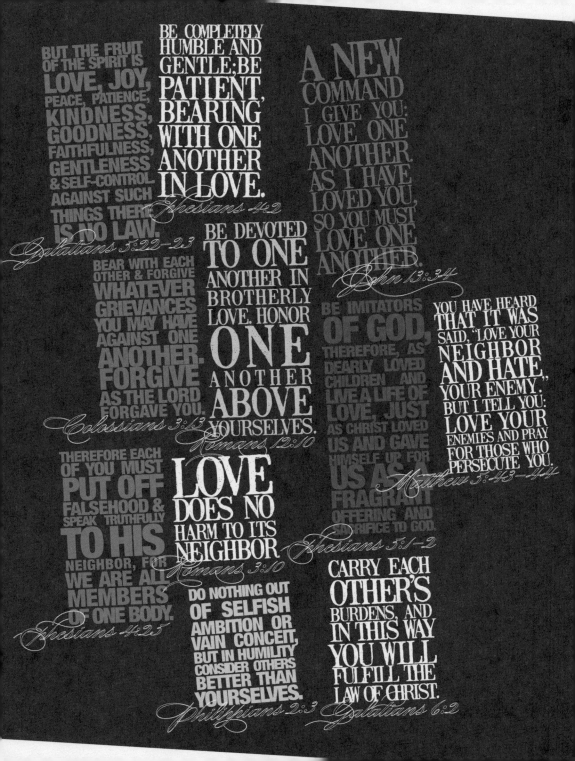

IF THE *world* KNOWS YOU ARE A *Christian* THEY LOOK TO YOU AND EXPECT YOU TO *represent* JESUS.

SO HERE'S THE QUESTION: WHEN THE WORLD LOOKS AT YOU DO THEY SEE JESUS?

If you are supposed to represent Jesus to the world, how do you do so? Do you show the world love, grace, mercy, kindness, humbleness, and joy? Or do you look out for your own interests above others'? Do you run people down? Do you dislike those who dislike you? You are called to love and to teach others to love. By loving those around you, you will draw them to Christ. And the world will see Christ in you.

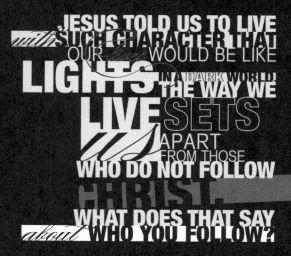

JESUS TOLD US TO LIVE *with* SUCH CHARACTER THAT OUR *lives* WOULD BE LIKE LIGHTS IN A DARK WORLD THE WAY WE LIVE SETS APART FROM THOSE WHO DO NOT FOLLOW CHRIST WHAT DOES THAT SAY *about* WHO YOU FOLLOW?

If you claim to be a Christ-follower, your life can do two things: it can push people away from God, or it can draw them near. If you claim to follow Christ and live just like everyone else, people look at you and figure that Jesus must not be that special. If you claim to follow Christ and live a life that matches God's expectations for you, people will notice the difference.

IF YOU LIVE A LIFE OF LOVE, SERVICE, HUMILITY, AND MERCY TOWARD BELIEVERS AND UNBELIEVERS ALIKE, PEOPLE WILL SEE YOUR LIFE AND BE DRAWN TO GOD.

IMAGINE WHAT WOULD HAPPEN IF YOU PICKED UP YOUR IPOD, PRESSED PLAY, AND KETCHUP CAME OUT. OR CONSIDER WHAT YOUR RESPONSE WOULD BE IF WHEN YOU PRESSED DOWN YOUR CAR'S GAS PEDAL, IT TURNED ON THE TV IN YOUR HOUSE. WANT ANOTHER ONE? OK, HOW WOULD YOU REACT IF YOU TURNED ON THE FAUCET TO POUR A GLASS OF WATER AND DOG FOOD CAME OUT? IF ANY OF THESE RIDICULOUS SITUATIONS ACTUALLY HAPPENED, YOU WOULD BE TOTALLY SHOCKED, AMAZED, AND POSSIBLY FRIGHTENED. WHY? SIMPLE: IT'S ALL ABOUT EXPECTATIONS.

YOU'D BE SHOCKED IF YOU TURNED ON YOUR IPOD AND KETCHUP CAME OUT BECAUSE YOU WOULDN'T EXPECT IT. THE NATURE OF AN IPOD IS SUCH THAT YOU HAVE COME TO EXPECT CERTAIN THINGS. BECAUSE AN IPOD'S ESSENTIAL NATURE IS THAT OF AN MP3 PLAYER, IT IS ONLY NATURAL THAT WHEN YOU PRESS PLAY, YOU HEAR MUSIC. YOU EXPECT THIS BECAUSE YOU KNOW IT IS THE NATURE OF AN IPOD.

Read 1 Peter 3:8–16. First Peter is actually a letter Peter wrote to Christians in several specific regions of the Roman Empire. These Christians were experiencing significant persecution because they claimed to follow Christ and only Christ. Peter wrote this letter to encourage and instruct them in their time of persecution. In verse 8, Peter made a statement that sums up the overall meaning of this passage. He said, "Finally, all of you, live in harmony with one another; be sympathetic, love as brothers, be compassionate and humble." The rest of the passage more or less supports this command from Peter: Live a good life. Do the right thing.

If you are a follower of Christ, you are called to live a life that separates you from the world around you. You must strive to get along with others, show sympathy for their circumstances and challenges, love them, care about their problems, and show them patience and kindness. Why? Because Christ lives in you. All of these actions serve to testify to the world why you are different. Your actions point to God.

Just like the essential nature of an iPod is to play music, your essential nature as a Christ-follower is to demonstrate Christ's love for the world through your right living.

CHRIST EXPECTS IT FROM YOU. ISN'T IT TIME YOU SHOWED THE WORLD THE DIFFERENCE HE HAS MADE IN YOUR LIFE?

PERSECUTION STORIES

This section is all about living a right life . . . a good life. Living a life of humility and kindness draws people to you. And when they get close enough, they learn that God is the source of your goodness.

This page serves as a simple reminder to you. You may think that living a good life is a drag. That it is boring. That it is much more fun to not worry about how you live. You might not worry about drawing people to God. After all, there are other Christians at your school, right?

Read these stories and realize that millions of people around the world make the decision to live a Christlike life . . . at the cost of their *own* lives.

THE COST OF *following*

Marzieh Amirizadeh Esmaeilabad and Maryam Rustampoor are not criminals. They are merely Christ-followers. But because of that simple fact they were arrested on March 5, 2009 by Iranian security forces.

Labeled "anti-government activists," the two women were sent to Evin Prison, a prison with the reputation of being a horrible place for women. They were allowed only a single one-minute phone call a day. Both women had serious health issues during their imprisonment.

Their only "crime" is believing and following Jesus.

Never GIVE UP

On February 8, 2009, a 79-year-old Chinese woman was released from prison. Shuang Shuying, a Christ-follower, had been imprisoned for two years due to her faith in Jesus. While imprisoned, she was harassed, interrogated and tortured by the Chinese government's Public Security Bureau. The day she was released, she immediately went to a hospital to tend to her gravely ill husband.

Through all her trials, Shuying never lost her faith in Christ. She prayed continuously during her ordeal. The Lord sustained her and gave her the strength to persevere.

Endangered

From November 2008 to January 2009, about 100 Christian men, women, and children were arrested in the country of Eritrea. Many of the captured Christians were taken to a military facility where they were severely abused. Many Christ-followers died due to untreated injuries that occurred while they were held captive.

The Eritrean government actively persecutes Christians. They are captured, tortured, and beaten in an attempt to deny their religious beliefs. Nearly 1,800 Eritrean Christians are believed to be under arrest simply because they follow Jesus.

Step 1 IS TO...

SHOW

Step 2 IS TO...

SHARE

Step 3 IS TO...

TEACH

Step 4 IS TO...

SERVE

YOU **CANNOT** *make* DISCIPLES OF THOSE **AROUND** YOU UNLESS YOU **VALUE THEIR** NEEDS ABOVE YOUR **OWN.** *This* IS WHAT IT MEANS TO SERVE.

REMIND YOURSELF OF THIS FACT: YOU SHOULD TREAT OTHERS WITH LOVE **NOT** BECAUSE **YOU HAVE TO...**

BUT BECAUSE YOU CARE ABOUT THEM.

THIS *Believe*...

ALWAYS BE PREPARED TO GIVE AN ANSWER TO EVERYONE WHO ASKS YOU TO
GIVE THE REASON FOR THE HOPE THAT YOU HAVE.—1 PETER 13:15

"BE PREPARED TO GIVE AN ANSWER."
When you stand up for something
you believe in, are you prepared to
give a reason why? When someone
asks you the tough questions about
your faith, are you prepared to answer
them? If your faith is important to you,
maybe it's time you actually sat down
and thought about what you believe.

What do you believe? For the following statements,
write a few sentences to explain why you believe what
you believe. If you have trouble, start a conversation
with an adult whom you trust.

IF YOU BELIEVE GOD IS THE ALL-POWERFUL CREATOR OF THE UNIVERSE, THEN EXPLAIN WHY.

IF YOU BELIEVE JESUS IS THE SON OF GOD, THEN EXPLAIN WHY.

IF YOU BELIEVE THE HOLY SPIRIT LIVES INSIDE YOU, THEN EXPLAIN WHY.

IF YOU BELIEVE JESUS OFFERS FORGIVENESS OF SINS AND ETERNAL LIFE, THEN EXPLAIN WHY.

IF YOU BELIEVE THAT ORDINARY PEOPLE—CHRIST-FOLLOWERS LIKE YOU—ARE GOD'S
PLAN TO TAKE HIS STORY OF LOVE AND FORGIVENESS TO THE ENTIRE WORLD, THEN
EXPLAIN WHY.

How'd you do? Did you find it hard to explain why you believe what you believe? Hopefully this makes you understand the importance of being prepared to help others understand why your faith is so important.

IF YOU DON'T KNOW WHAT YOU BELIEVE, HOW CAN YOU SHARE IT WITH OTHERS?

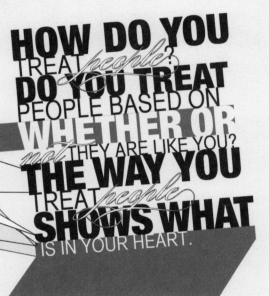

HOW DO YOU TREAT *people*? DO YOU TREAT PEOPLE BASED ON WHETHER OR *not* THEY ARE LIKE YOU? THE WAY YOU TREAT *people* SHOWS WHAT IS IN YOUR HEART.

When you put yourself out there, when you take a stand for what you believe, you open yourself up to people making fun of you. Has this ever happened to you? If so, how did you treat those people? Did you get angry? Upset? Did you act like you were better than them? The truth is that if you are a Christ-follower, you must treat all people with mercy—especially those who do not believe in Jesus, or who reject your attempts to share your faith.

EXTENDING MERCY TO THOSE WHO REJECT YOU MAY BE THE BEST WAY TO SHOW THEM THE DIFFERENCE CHRIST HAS MADE IN YOUR LIFE.

FREE WRITING

That's right . . . One more chance to take a turn at free-writing! (Some of you are cheering . . . some of you are groaning.) Let's recall the instructions one more time. In free-writing you get a prompt and then you begin writing. Don't pause, don't think about what you are going to write before you write it . . . just write. Remember how it's done? Cool .

And now, time for your prompt: When you have taken a stand for Christ in your life, you probably have experienced some resistance. How have you dealt with people who don't believe in Jesus, or who might have even acted hostile toward you because you do believe in Jesus? Why is it hard to show mercy to those against us? And what does mercy mean to you, anyway?

Now DON'T hesitate . . . GET WRITING!

AS WE WRAP up

THIS SECTION ON WHAT IT MEANS TO BE A **DISCIPLE-MAKER,** let's REMEMBER SOMETHING **PAUL** HAD TO SAY ABOUT **HOW** WE CONDUCT OURSELVES.

PAUL SAID IN JUDE 21–22 THAT WE ARE TO REMAIN IN GOD'S LOVE AND MERCY AS WE LIVE THIS LIFE, BUT THAT WE ARE ALSO TO ACT IN MERCY TOWARD OTHERS. PAUL SAID WE ARE TO BE MERCIFUL TO THOSE AROUND US WHO HAVE QUESTIONS ABOUT THE CHRISTIAN LIFE.

THAT'S TWO MERCIES IN TWO VERSES. SEEMS LIKE PAUL WAS TRYING TO TELL US SOMETHING.

LET'S TAKE A QUICK LOOK AT WHAT IT MEANS.

THE WORD MERCIFUL AS IT APPEARS IN JUDE 22 IS THE GREEK WORD, **ELEEMON** (PRONOUNCED, EL-EH-**AY**-MONE).

THE WORD MEANS: **"TO BE ACTIVELY COMPASSIONATE; TO HAVE FEELINGS OF PITY WITH A FOCUS OF SHOWING LOVE AND COMPASSION TO THOSE IN NEED."**

WOW . . . NOW THAT IS QUITE A WORD. LET'S THINK FOR A MOMENT ABOUT HOW YOU CAN APPLY THE DEFINITION IN YOUR WORLD.

Let's start by defining what it means to be in need. Name some different needs people have that might inspire compassion from you.

Now, think about what you listed above. The word for merciful implies "active" compassion. For each of the needs you listed above, write down at least one possible thing you could do to help address the specific need.

Finally, think about this: the most important need in a person's life is the need to know Jesus Christ. Think about what it means to show mercy to those who do not believe, or still have questions about their faith. Then, write a prayer below asking God to help you feel mercy toward these people.

Conversation LOG

HOW YOU DEAL WITH PEOPLE IS IMPORTANT. AFTER ALL, IF YOU WANT TO LEAD PEOPLE TO BECOME DISCIPLES OF CHRIST, YOU HAVE TO TREAT THEM WITH RESPECT. IF YOU DON'T, PEOPLE PROBABLY WON'T GIVE YOU A CHANCE TO MAKE A DIFFERENCE IN THEIR LIVES.

This page is a conversation log. The idea is for you to stop at the end of each day for the next week and record one meaningful conversation you had that day. Record whether you had a chance to be merciful to someone. Write down when you had a chance to show mercy but failed. Also, write down circumstances where you successfully showed mercy and kindness to someone.

CONVERSATION LOG

DAY 1

DAY 2

DAY 3

DAY 4

DAY 5

DAY 6

DAY 7

Step 1 IS TO...
SHOW

Step 2 IS TO...
SHARE

Step 3 IS TO...
TEACH

Step 4 IS TO...
SERVE

Step 5
MERCY

AS YOU journey THROUGH THE DISCIPLE-MAKING PROCESS, YOU MUST DEAL MERCIFULLY WITH BOTH THOSE WHO believe IN CHRIST AND, DO NOT believe IN CHRIST. SHOW THE WORLD THE KINDNESS, PATIENCE, AND LOVE OF CHRIST.

DEVOTION

HAVE YOU EVER HEARD THE PHRASE, "LIKE A FISH TRYING TO SWIM UPSTREAM"?

A FISH SWIMMING DOWNSTREAM HAS IT EASY. A FISH'S BODY IS DESIGNED TO MAKE MINIMAL RESISTANCE IN THE WATER. THE CURRENT PROPELS IT FORWARD. WITH JUST THE LIGHTEST BIT OF WORK, IT CAN BASICALLY CRUISE THE STREAM WITHOUT A CARE IN THE WORLD, GLIDING ON THE FORCE OF THE WATER.

BUT A FISH SWIMMING UPSTREAM HAS IT PRETTY BAD. IT HAS TO FIGHT TWICE AS HARD TO GET ANYWHERE. THE CURRENT IS WORKING AGAINST IT, RESISTING ITS EVERY MOVE. EVERYTHING IS WORKING AGAINST IT. AND YOU CAN ONLY IMAGINE HOW IT FEELS WHEN ONE OF ITS NEIGHBORS GOES ZIPPING BY, HEADED DOWN-STREAM, JUST GOING WITH THE FLOW . . .

Read Jude 17–22. Jude was written by Jesus and James' half-brother. The Book of Jude is all about swimming upstream. It is a letter written to Christians who found themselves going against a hostile world. The passage you just read speaks to this fact. Jude said that there will be people who doubt you and make fun of you. (This is what the "scoffers" means.) Not only did James say that Christians are to stay strong in the face of the scoffers, he said we are to show mercy to those who question our way of life.

As a follower of Christ in this world, you are a fish swimming upstream. You are fighting the current of a world that will only hate and make fun of you. But Jude said that you couldn't retaliate, you couldn't ignore them. He said you have to be merciful to those who have questions and bring the message of Jesus to those who have not heard it.

This is easier said than done. But as a follower of Christ, you don't have a choice. It comes with the territory. See, God's plan since the beginning of time was for you to lead people to Him. By showing understanding and mercy mixed with the truth of God's Word, you show people the way to life in God.

Swimming upstream might be hard. But it's worth the fight.

Other than the fact that the Holy Spirit is God, somehow part of the mysterious Trinity, we don't often talk about Him. Today, He is often reduced to little more then a theological point to check off some list for church membership. "Yes, I believe in God the Father, Son, and Holy Spirit. . . Check." But God's Spirit is a vital part of our lives as Christ-followers. This is God's gift of life, truth, and power.

Maybe talk of the Holy Ghost has sounded too mystical or even spooky to you in the past. Don't write this off as something to merely believe or as an influence reserved for goofy behavior and religious extremes. You need Him. This is the One, True, Living God; all-powerful and all-knowing. Get to know Him (He already knows you).

Session 1   We Have the Power—Pg 164-169

Session 2   Another Helper—Pg 170-175

Session 3   How Can We Know?—Pg 176-181

Session 4   The Big Show—Pg 182-187

Session 5   The Confidence Of Certainty—Pg 188-193

Session 6   Guide to Life—Pg 194-199

IT'S EVERYWHERE.

You probably don't even realize how often you respond to it.

Sometimes a conscious effort is made to seek it out, but usually it goes unnoticed.

Routine and habit take over and the fact that it's present never crosses your mind as long as everything is working the way you want.

Sure you recognize it, but what is it really?

WHY IS IT WHAT IT IS?

Maybe you have an idea, maybe even a good idea.

But whether you can confidently explain the nature of its existence, you know what it represents.

POWER.

(Reread this page, but instead of just seeing a circle with a vertical line, think about the Holy Spirit. Think about the Holy Spirit every time you see the POWER symbol today.)

Spirit = ?

This page is all yours. Write anything and everything you know about the Holy Spirit. If you want, you can also draw your own representation or symbol, but try to incorporate all of your thoughts. Who is the Spirit? What does He do? How have you experienced Him?

_____

Advocate **Breath** Breath of life Breath of the Almighty COMFORTER Comp
victs Counselor Dove Draws *Empowers* Eternal Spirit Fills **Gift** Go
Spirit Guarantees Guides Helper Holy Spirit Indwells Intercedes INVITES
Parakletos Pneuma **Power of the Most High** Regenerates Rer
news Ruwach SEALS Speaks Spirit Spirit of burning Spirit of Christ Spirit
Spirit of glory Spirit of God Spirit of grace Spirit of holiness Spirit of judgm
of justice Spirit of knowledge Spirit of love Spirit of power S
prophecy Spirit of revelation **Spirit of righteous**ness SPIRIT OF SELF-CONT
of sonship Spirit of the Father Spirit of the Son SPIRIT OF TRUTH Spirit of wisdom *Strer*
SWORD Teaches Testifies The Spirit is life Third person of the
Tongues of fire Washes **Wind** Advocate **Breath** Breath of life Breath of the
Comforter Compels Convicts Counselor Dove *Draws* Empowers *ETERNA*
Fills Gift God Good Spirit Guarantees Guides HELPER Holy Spirit Indwells
Invites LEADS Parakletos Pneuma Power of the Most High Regenerates R
Renews Ruwach Seals *Speaks* Spirit Spirit of burning Spirit of Christ S
counsel Spirit of glory Spirit of God Spirit of grace Spirit of holine
of judgment Spirit of justice *Spirit of knowledge* Spirit of love Spirit of power **Spirit o**
ecy Spirit of revelation Spirit of righteousness Spirit of self-control Spirit of sonship
the Father SPIRIT OF THE SON Spirit of truth Spirit of wis
STRENGTHENS Sword Teaches Testifies The Spirit is life Third per
Trinity Tongues of fire WASHES Wind Advocate *Breath* Breath of life B
Almighty **Comforter** Compels Convicts Counselor Dove Draws Empowers
Spirit Fills Gift God **GOOD SPIRIT** Guarantees Guides Helper Holy Sp
Intercedes Invites Leads Parakletos **Pneuma** Power of the Most High REC
ATES Reminds Renews Ruwach *Seals* Speaks Spirit *Spirit of burning* Sp
Spirit of counsel Spirit of glory Spirit of God **SPIRIT OF GRACE** Spi
ness Spirit of judgment SPIRIT OF JUSTICE Spirit of knowledge Spirit of love
power Spirit of prophecy Spirit of revelation *Spirit of righteous*

Devotion

Have you ever traveled on an international flight? Tons of people from different cultures get crammed into the same space. The airliner's cabin is jam-packed with different fashions, languages, manners . . . smells. But regardless of any cultural differences among the passengers, most of them have one thing in common after they finally settle into their seats. Other than the snack and beverage cart, anticipation for the in-flight movie consumes the thoughts of young and old alike.

Sure, some people tune it out, disregarding the entertainment beaming from overhead monitors; but most of the captive audience is paying some attention. Here's the coolest part: Everyone is watching the same thing, but the headphones allow each individual to hear his or her own language. It can be pretty amusing to scan the channels and hear some well-known actor overdubbed in different dialects.

On a much greater scale, this is similar to what happened in Acts 2. People from all over the ancient world had gathered in Jerusalem during Pentecost. Christ had recently ascended into the clouds, and now the disciples were huddled together, eagerly awaiting the arrival of the Holy Spirit.

Read Acts 2:1–8.

Acts 2 describes the beginning of the Church. Imagine the sound of jet engines inside your house. The Spirit lands on each Christ-follower, floating like a flame, a burning light above each person's head. Empowered by the Holy Spirit, everyone rushes outside and begins sharing God's story. Miraculously, people from different cultures hear the stories in their native language. Seventeen different people groups are named in verses 9–11.

Now read the reactions in verses 12–18.

The scene caught some people's undivided attention. Others tuned out. Peter explained that the time had finally come for God to begin working in a new way among His people. The power of God had poured out on all people, regardless of ethnicity, age, or gender. The Holy Spirit was and is doing incredible things for all who will follow Christ.

The bottom line is now that the Spirit has arrived, empowering God's people, we're all in this thing together. Are you ready for the trip of a lifetime?

Let's get to know our invisible friend. Though we can't see Him, the Holy Spirit is not imaginary. We're not talking about some fictional companion such as one a young child would conjure up. Technically, God dreamed us up and His Spirit was involved in the creative process.

Look at the very first two verses of your Bible (Gen. 1:1–2). When nothing existed, God's Spirit was in motion. The Hebrew word for spirit here is *ruwach*, which can also mean "wind or breath." (Say it out loud; it even sounds like a swirling wind.) Imagine God taking a deep breath, and then the words "Let there be . . ." come rushing through the universe.

Whoa. So the Spirit is nothing new. Not only was the Spirit there at the creation of the world, He is later involved in another miraculous beginning. . . Turn to the first book of the New Testament. Read Matthew 1:18–25. What new beginning is described here?

Both Mary and Joseph trusted God in this unbelievable situation. The new life that was literally birthed from this teenage girl was the promised Messiah of the Old Testament, the One who would bring new life to all who worship Him.

With that thought, let's check out two more beginnings. You just read in Matthew that the LORD spoke about Jesus through the prophets. Read 2 Peter 1:19–21. What new beginning is described here?

Since it came from God, not humanity, verse 19 says we should pay careful attention to God's Word until our lives and all of creation is transformed.

Finally, what new beginning is described in John 3:5–8?

For you to experience a new beginning—life with God—you must be born of the Spirit, too. This birth is supernatural, but we're not talking about a physical miracle here. Being born again, or born from above, is a spiritual birth into God's Kingdom. Obviously you've been born physically (of water/flesh), but have you been born spiritually (of the Spirit)?

Look back over the four beginnings in which the Holy Spirit was actively involved. Remember, this is just the beginning! But what better place to start? Creation, Jesus, Scripture, Salvation. . . That's a really impressive list. It's time to get to know Him. The Holy Spirit is constantly at work, on the move, breathing new life into things. So, pray right now that He would open your eyes to the new things God wants to do in your life, starting today.

"You will receive power when the Holy Spirit comes on you; and you will be my witnesses in Jerusalem, and in all Judea and Samaria, and to the ends of the earth." — Acts 1:8

⚠ ATTENTION ⚠

You have God inside of you.

Continue Crash Deep down Dwell Employ Endure Engage Engross Es
XIST Fill FRIEND Hang in Hang one's hat Hang out House Immerse Indwell
Interior Into Locate *Lodge* Make one's home *Near* Nest Occupy Park Per
e Possess Present Quarter Remain Reside Rest with **Room** Roommate Roost So
ttle Shelter Soak Sojourn Squat Stay Take up Temple Tenant Tent Vital *Within*
oany Aide Ally **ANIMATE** Attend Bear with **BREATHE** Bunk Close *Comp*
mrade Continue Crash *Deep down* Dwell Employ Endure Engage **Engross** Establish
nd Hang in *Hang one's hat* Hang out **House** Immerse Indwell Inhabit Inside
ocate Lodge Make one's home Near Nest Occupy Park *Perch* Populate F
resent Quarter Remain Reside Rest with ROOM Roommate Roost SATURATE
Soak Sojourn Squat Stay TAKE UP Temple Tenant Tent Vital Within A
MPANY Aide Ally Animate Attend Bear with Breathe Bunk Close Companion Co
e Crash Deep DOWN Dwell Employ ENDURE Engage Engross Establi
Friend Hang in Hang one's hat Hang out House *Immerse* Indwell **Inhabit** Inside
OCATE Lodge The Spirit lives WITH you and IN you. M
nome Near Nest Occupy Park Perch Populate Possess *Present* Quarter R
Rest with Room Roommate **Roost** Saturate Settle Shelter Soak Sojourn
AKE UP Temple Tenant Tent Vital Within **Abide** Accompany Aide Ally Anim
AR WITH Breathe Bunk *Close* Companion COMRADE Continue Crash **Deep down**

Employ **En**
Engage Eng
Establish Ex
Fill Friend H
in Hang on
HANG OUT
Immerse In
Inhabit Insid
Into LOCATE
Make o
home

ccupy *Park* Perch Populate POSSESS Present Quarter Remain **Reside**
Roommate Roost Saturate Settle **Shelter** Soak Sojourn Squat Stay Take up T
Tenant Tent *VITAL* Within Abide Accompany Aide *Ally* Animate Attend

Did You Hear That?

You've seen the little cartoons: the angel and the devil. They both sit on a shoulder whispering into your ears, either encouraging you to do what's right or tempting you to act selfishly. As Christ-followers we have something greater than a little cartoon on our shoulders, we literally have God inside of us!

Have you ever felt like God's Spirit was telling you to do something (or to not do something)? Write about it here.

When did you ignore or rely on the Holy Spirit?

What was happening?

What made you think that God might be trying to tell you something?

Did you ignore or trust that feeling?

What was the result?

If you've never "heard" the Holy Spirit, ask yourself why not? Are you listening?

POWER SOURCE

The guy who wrote more books of the Bible than anyone was far from perfect. He wasn't involved in all the big, nasty sins that plagued his culture—and ours; he had a different kind of story. As an incredibly religious person, Paul was formerly filled with pride and self-righteousness. Saul (his name at the time) had the most advanced theological education possible and his passion for strict Jewish Law was unsurpassed. While on his own personal crusade against the newly established Church, imprisoning Christ-followers and seeing them put to death, Saul had a life-changing encounter with Jesus (so much so that he changed his name from Saul to Paul). Unaware that He had actually been an enemy of God, attacking Christ's Church, Paul then championed the gospel of grace and freedom in the Spirit.

Read Romans 8:1–11. What has the Spirit done for you according to verses 1–2?

What does Paul say in verses 7–8 about our natural desires?

What about a mind set on the Spirit?

Paul had completely devoted his life to the Law. He thought he could simply make up his mind to live by all the rules and please God. After hearing the voice of God, however, Paul realized it was impossible to perfectly submit to the Law. He was condemned by the very Law that he used to justify killing and imprisoning Christ-followers . . . in God's name! Only the Spirit of life could set him free.

Look back at this life-changing power in verses 9–11.

Regardless of what Paul thought about his relationship with God before yielding to the Holy Spirit, what does he say about the Spirit in verse 9? What difference does the Spirit make in your life?

Take a minute to stop and really think about this fact. This is HUGE. How much power do you think it took to resurrect Jesus? Verse 11 says that the very same power that raised Christ from the dead is inside of you! The same power! What are you doing with this power?

While you let that soak in, jump over to Paul's first letter to the church in Corinth. Read 1 Corinthians 6:19–20 and then rewrite it here, replacing "you/your" with "I/me/my."

Devotion

Twinkie. What first comes to mind when you hear the word Twinkie? You probably don't think about its practically infinite shelf life, or wonder why Hostess® dressed the snack cake up like a cowboy (Twinkie the Kid) for advertising. Seriously, who can imagine some dude at the rodeo pulling a Twinkie from the back pocket of his Wranglers®? Before your mind wanders to any of those things, you instantly think "cream-filled sponge cake."

A Twinkie wouldn't be a Twinkie without its filling. What if after unwrapping your treat you bite into a hollow finger of yellow fluff. Your horror swells, as nobody around you seems to care; "it's still a Twinkie," they disregard. "NO IT ISN'T!" you scream. OK . . . Maybe that's a little melodramatic. But even if you didn't get that emotional over some cake missing its filling, you can't deny that by definition, a Twinkie is a cream-filled sponge cake. Without the filling, it isn't really a Twinkie at all, no matter what it looks like from the outside.

Check out John 14:15–17. Jesus was explaining to His disciples what life looks like for people who truly love Him. We will obey His commands if we love Christ. Don't get overwhelmed; Jesus explained that He wasn't just giving us a list of rules to follow to prove our sincerity. He was giving us a helper—the Helper. By definition, Christ-followers have the Holy Spirit with them and inside of them. The Spirit will help you love Christ and keep His commands.

Why doesn't it freak us out when people act like it's no big deal to call themselves "Christians" without being filled with the Holy Spirit? All the time people say things like, "So-and-so is a Christian, he/she just doesn't live like it." Christ said that if we love Him, we will live like it. We will obey His Word. His Spirit will always be with us and in us to help. Right now, be totally honest with yourself. If someone heard your name, what would come to mind? Would they immediately define you as a Spirit-filled follower of Christ? Or has your life been hollow fluff?

"He saved us, not because of righteous things we had done, but because of his mercy. He saved us through the washing of rebirth and renewal by the Holy Spirit."— Titus 3:5

reverb
reverb
reverb
175

REMEMBER TODAY:

Love Christ by Keeping
His Commands

Every day, you find yourself in all kinds of places and situations. Use these pictures and Scriptures to begin training yourself to listen to the Spirit no matter where you are or what you are doing. Think about your own life: your schedule and the people with whom you cross paths. WHAT IS THE SPIRIT SAYING TO YOU?

Where is the Spirit reminding you, "Be still and know that I am God"?

For whom is the Spirit reminding you, "Whatever you did for the least of these, you did for Me"?

Why is the Spirit reminding you, "Look at what He has created; if God cares for all of this, will He not take care of you? Don't worry about your clothes and stuff." What else is He saying to you right now?

When is the Spirit reminding you, "There is no greater love than to give your life for your friends"?

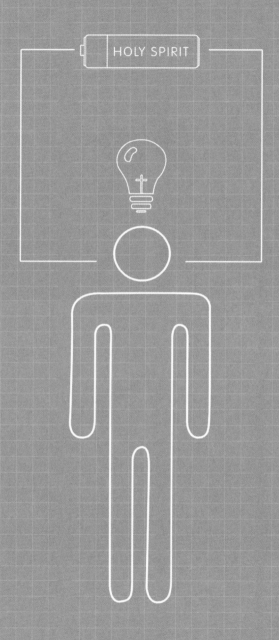

MORE THAN A BENEFIT

In case nobody ever told you, or maybe to correct something you've heard, following Christ doesn't guarantee a happy and successful life (not on a worldly scale, at least). Sorry to burst your bubble, but God's chief concern is not your feeling good about yourself, thinking positive, and having financial blessings. Yes, abundant life is promised; but it isn't about feelings and possessions. Our Bible is quite convincing to the fact that God's people often endure hardship, oppression, and poverty. God's primary concern for us is His glory through salvation and the advancement of the Kingdom of Heaven. Any time one kingdom invades another conflict is inevitable. The world will not give way without a fight.

The Holy Spirit is not only a benefit; He is a necessity. We wouldn't make it through this life, not in a way that honored our King and pleased the Judge, without the Spirit as our constant companion.

Read Mark 13:5–13.

Verses 5–6 warn you of false teachings about Christ. What dangerous or misleading beliefs and opinions about Jesus are you aware of today?

How do you "watch out" so that you are not deceived?

Regardless of all the terrible things going on in the world (war; natural disasters; broken families; legal, political, and religious persecution) what should be our focus according to verse 10?

Christ tells us not to worry, despite the hardships we will endure. According to verse 11, how is it possible to have peace in the midst of chaos?

In order to recognize spiritual attack, find peace in God's promises, and proclaim the gospel while empowered by the Holy Spirit, you obviously have to know the Word. This is your only weapon in spiritual warfare; the sword of the Spirit is the Word of God (Eph. 6:17). Write down a time that you will commit to reading your Bible on a regular basis.

Pray for the Holy Spirit to be your strength as you walk through trials (Zech. 4:6).
Pray that the promises of God's Word will be your peace (Eph. 1:13–14).
Pray that you will testify boldly, no matter what (Isa. 61:1–3).
How will you help preach the gospel to all nations?

Devotion

So what do you do when you really want to remember something? Do you write it on your hand? (Parents love that.) Maybe your trick is an alarm on your cell or iCal? Or are you old school and keep an organizer? Ever use a dry-erase marker on your mirror? Do you keep your inbox full of texts and emails that you read over and over as a reminder of what a boyfriend or girlfriend has said? Do you harass your friends, siblings, or parents, repeatedly saying, "don't let me forget . . . seriously." Well, what if they aren't around? If it's really super-important, how do you make sure that you won't forget?

Read John 14:23–27. Jesus told His disciples that He would not always be with them. They had spent a lot of time together, maybe three years at this point. By now, even though they don't fully realize who Jesus is and what He will do for everyone, they know that this relationship is something special. The disciples have given everything to follow Christ, learn from His teachings, and follow His example. The thought of Him leaving seems stressful to say the least.

Christ promises that we don't have to worry about forgetting what He said and did. We can experience His unconditional peace by trusting His Word. The Holy Spirit is the ultimate reminder. When we keep His commands, it shows our love for God. The Spirit is our Helper and Teacher. He doesn't just lecture us with a bunch of information; He is with us every step of the way, showing us what it all means and how to apply what we're learning. Maybe something pops into your mind, or you read your Bible and understand it in a new way—that's the Holy Spirit. Sometimes you find yourself in a situation and suddenly find just the right words or know exactly how to respond. That's Him. Whatever your situation, don't worry. He's always with you. Listen to Him.

"As soon as Jesus was baptized, he went up out of the water. At that moment heaven was opened, and he saw the Spirit of God descending like a dove and lighting on him."　— Matthew 3:16

Devotion

Reduce. Reuse. Recycle. These are good principles. To reduce, we live thoughtfully, practicing self-control and moderation. To reuse, we get creative, meeting various needs with the resources already at our disposal. And if trash can't be avoided . . . recycling takes old things, stripping away the impurities, and creates something entirely new.

Take a look at the recycling logo. The triangle is made up of three identical arrows pointing from one to the next. It's a great modern image of the holy Trinity. God is one, like the triangle; He is also three, like the arrows. Just as no arrow is bigger than another, neither is God the Father, Son, or Holy Spirit any greater or less than the other. They are all God.

In John 15:26–16:4, among other places, we catch a glimpse of the mysterious nature of the Trinity. Keep in mind the picture of the recycling logo while you read verses 26–27. Visualize Jesus as the bottom left arrow in the logo, God the Father up top, and His Spirit in us on the right. Christ is in the process of explaining that His time on earth is coming to an end; He will soon go up to the Father. Jesus promised to send the Holy Spirit down from the Father to the disciples. The Holy Spirit would then testify about Christ. When the Spirit points people to Christ, Jesus points them to the Father, who sends the Spirit to people. Do you see the cycle?

Jesus went on to clarify in 16:1–4 that life was about to get messy. Since the world would try to rid itself of Christ and His followers, God sent us the Helper, the Spirit of Truth. He will enable us to live thoughtfully, keeping the commands of Jesus in mind. Christ-followers are expected to live set apart from a world full of garbage. Everything we have can be used to point people to the love of Christ. Once that starts happening, our lives get caught up in an endless cycle of testifying to the redeeming power of God. He takes our lives, cleanses us from sin, and makes us brand new.

When was the last time you shared your testimony?

Don't let the word "testimony" intimidate you. Often we think a person needs some Hollywood drama to have a good testimony. Don't buy that lie! If you have been born again, made brand new through the work of the Holy Spirit in your life, you have a GREAT testimony. Remember, you have the power of the resurrection, the Holy Spirit, dwelling inside of you! Don't you think people need to know? Don't you want them to experience life transformation, too?

You're not writing a script, just some key moments when you have experienced God's power. These can come up in all kinds of conversations with different people in different places.

What is the most amazing God-experience you have ever had?

Describe how you first knew that you had a personal relationship with God?

How would you describe a relationship with God?

What difference does it make to have the Holy Spirit in your life?

From what sins has Christ freed you?

When has He comforted you in pain/suffering/sadness?

Imagine conversations you may have with each person on this page. How could the Spirit speak through you to them? Are there certain people you feel more or less comfortable talking to in real life?

A physician named Luke wrote two books in the New Testament: Luke and Acts. The purpose of these books is to provide details about the life and ministry of Jesus while He was on earth and then of His Spirit through the Church after He left. Like any good doctor, Luke took careful notes. Here we will look at two death records: the death of Jesus on the cross, and the death of Stephen, the first Christian martyr. Read Luke 23:32–47.

Jesus has just spoken prophetic words of warning and judgment on the daughters of Jerusalem (vv. 28–31). Then, He was lead out of the city for execution (v. 32). A violent mob hurled insults at Him (vv. 35–37). What three things did Jesus say while being executed?

(v. 34)

(v. 43)

(v. 46)

Once Jesus had said this, He breathed his last breath (v. 46). And finally, people mourned and scattered while Jesus was buried (vv. 47–53).

Now turn over to Acts 7:51–60 and read about Stephen.

Stephen had just spoken prophetic words of warning and judgment against the brothers and fathers in Jerusalem (vv. 1–52). Then, he was lead out of the city for execution (v. 58). A violent mob hurled insults at Him (vv. 54, 57). What three things did Stephen say while being executed?

(v. 56)

(v. 59)

(v. 60)

Once Stephen had said this, he fell asleep (v. 60). And finally, people mourned and scattered while Stephen was buried (Acts 8:1–4).

The key to Stephen's testimony is that he is FULL OF THE HOLY SPIRIT. God's Spirit empowered Stephen to speak and act just like Christ! Are you so full of God's power that you boldly stand up for His truth, even when it is unpopular or may carry severe consequences? Do you resemble Christ this closely?

Now check this out. . . Notice the places to which people were scattered after Stephen's death (Acts 8:1). Even in this tragic event, the Spirit is at work, fulfilling Jesus' final words before leaving the disciples (Acts 1:8).

No matter what your circumstance, the Holy Spirit will empower you to testify to the truth of Christ. Things may not turn out the way you would hope, but God is working out His plan.

"They saw what seemed to be tongues of fire that separated and came to rest on each of them. All of them were filled with the Holy Spirit and began to speak in other tongues as the Spirit enabled them." — Acts 2:3–4

a new season
of renewable energy
for the next generation

Devotion

Remember those little plastic capsules you played with as a child? You would drop them in hot water and watch as the plastic casing melted away. A mysterious surprise emerged, slowly taking shape until you recognized some foam creature. It wouldn't work if you refused to drop it; you had to let go of it first. You also couldn't help it along; it would tear to pieces if you attempted to free the sopping substance from its gummy cocoon.

Read John 16:5–11. Christ explained to His disciples that they had to let Him go. Not that He was fragile or anything would be ruined, but that God's design required a time of transition. Earlier in John's Gospel, Jesus had taught that like a seed, His body would be sacrificed in order to introduce new life in the Spirit. Like a seed, we too must die to ourselves, shedding our flesh, to allow the Spirit to produce fruit that glorifies the Father.

There is no short cut. There is no way around God's plan. Just like Christ submitted to the will of God, so must we. Since Jesus is no longer with us on earth, His Spirit has been sent to help us in this life. We can be confident in three things as the Spirit slowly reveals the nature of God's character (and ours).

First, we know that sinful desires must be shed, replaced by trust in Christ. His Spirit will convict us of what needs to go and what needs to grow. Second, we know that His Spirit will empower us to live by faith, reminding us of what Christ said and did. The Helper will nurture spiritual health, becoming the righteousness of Christ in us. Finally, we should feel confident knowing that God is not abandoning us, nor can evil overcome us. God is in control. He is doing a new thing and His power is more than sufficient.

MORE THAN FIRE INSURANCE

The fact that we are set free from the Law, redeemed by Christ, does not mean we are free to do whatever we want. In Paul's day, just as today, some people misunderstood his message and treated the gospel of grace as a "Get Out of Jail Free" card. Believing in Jesus was fire insurance, essentially. As long as they believed Jesus was the Son of God they could live however they wanted, and God would forgive them, letting them into heaven when they died.

In Galatians 5:13–25, Paul set the record straight. Go ahead and read it now, praying for God to convict you of any sin and for His Spirit to lead you into confident action. In light of verses 13–15, how have you abused your freedom in Christ? Write down examples of ways you indulge your sinful desires.

Paul taught that because of God's grace, we should be free to serve others, sharing God's love. This is not necessarily easy. When reading between the lines, we recognize Paul was pointing out that "church people" could be really ugly and backbiting. Do you think the Church still has this problem today? If so, how can it be remedied?

Earlier in this chapter, Paul used the common expression "yoke of slavery" to describe the relationship to sin from which we have been released. A yoke was a wooden beam that bound animals, or even people, together as they worked. Beginning with verse 16, Paul explained that if we were truly bound to the Spirit, being lead by Him, then we would walk with Him and be productive in His work. It is completely unreasonable to assume that you can be yoked to sinful desires, yet also with the Spirit of a holy God. They are heading in opposite directions, reaping different harvests.

Read the list of visible evidence for a life lead by a sinful nature in verses 19–21.
Now, write down the things that, like weeds, you can't seem to root out of your life.

Be honest about this list; Scripture is clear about the nature of this rotten fruit.

Now read about the fruit of the Spirit in verses 22–23. Notice it doesn't say fruits (plural). We can't pick and choose which of these best fit our lifestyles. Everything on this list is part of the same fruit. If the Spirit has root in your life, visible fruit will develop for all to see.

Pray over this list; which are most evident in your life?

Which pieces are underdeveloped or missing all together?

the
fruit
OF
the
Spirit
IS
LOVE,
joy,
peace,
patience,
kindness,
goodness,
FAITHFULNESS,
gentleness,
self-control.

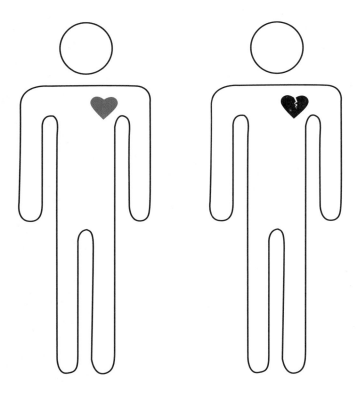

LORD God, You alone are good. Your Word is true. You are all-knowing, all-powerful, always present, and always fair. There is none like You. Nothing comes even close. You created everything, and You hold it all together. The past, present, and future are in Your hands. You are in control. Forgive me for trying to take control of my own life. Forgive me for trying to control others. Forgive me for allowing junk to distract and consume me. Forgive me for choosing to put other things in Your rightful place. Forgive me for my selfish motives and sinful desires. Thank You that Jesus Christ has saved me from myself. Thank You that He took the punishment I deserve. Thank you for Your mercy and grace. I will live for You today and every day. I can only do this with Your help and by Your power working through me. Fill me with Your Holy Spirit. Create in me a clean heart and renew a right spirit within me. I love You. I need You. I ask You, in Your name. **Amen.**

"The one who sows to please his sinful nature, from that nature will reap destruction; the one who sows to please the Spirit, from the Spirit will reap eternal life."
— Galatians 6:8

A CAMERA DOES NOT CHOOSE WHAT PICTURES IT WILL TAKE;
IT IS DIRECTED BY SOMEONE BEHIND THE LENS.

The wonder of a photograph is not that it was produced of its own will,
for it wasn't, but that it possesses an ability to reveal truth and beauty by
focusing your attention on someone else's unique perspective.

Likewise, the Holy Spirit illuminates God's way of seeing things.

HE OPENS OUR EYES TO HIS GLORY.

Devotion

Waves crash, soaking you to the bone as you jam your sandaled feet under the side of the raft. You white-knuckle the T-grip of your paddle, hanging on for dear life as the momentum never stops. Everything is swirling and churning . . . a constant battle to suck you under, hurl you into the air, or sweep you away. White water rafting is one of the greatest adrenaline rushes you can experience.

What gives you the confidence to plunge down the snaking river with little more than an inflated piece of rubber and sticks of plastic? Even a boat full of beginners can make it safely through the rapids with the help of a leader. A professional river guide knows every inch of your journey. He or she knows the unseen dangers and the right speed and direction needed to hit all of the currents in order to have a safe and fun trip. As long as you trust the instructions called out and respond accordingly, not only will everything be fine, it will be an incredible adventure.

Read John 16:12–15. The Holy Spirit knows everything that you'll ever need to know as you journey through life. He's not just making things up on the fly; He's telling you precisely what the Creator needs you to know. You can trust Him; He'll never steer you wrong.

Like a river guide, God isn't going to overwhelm you with details of your entire journey. Once you're on board with where He is headed, He'll give you some basic instructions. You'd freak out if you knew everything you would face; but as you go, your confidence in the Spirit's guidance will grow, your response time to His direction will quicken, and you'll make it through any rough waters. Your life is rushing past. Whatever it is that tries to suck you down, knock you out, or carry you away, know that you don't have to go with the flow. Trust the Spirit God has given you and life will be an incredible adventure.

Questions

It's OK. Jesus said you would have questions. Life gets complicated. It's confusing. Nobody expects you to have all the answers. Not knowing everything doesn't make you a bad person or a bad Christian. When following an infinite God, you're bound to encounter things you just can't wrap your mind around.

Write down any questions you have about God, life, death, salvation, faith, eternity, morality, relationships, the Bible, whatever . . . There are no limits here.

Here's the great news: His Spirit will guide you into all truth. He gives understanding, wisdom, and perfect advice. The Holy Spirit is your counselor, advocate, teacher, and guide. Listen to Him. Trust Him. Follow Him—wherever He may lead, even if you don't understand. You may never fully understand in this life. But He will never lead you astray. He will never leave nor forsake you. He cannot tempt or lie. He is perfectly good.

Questions I have -

Scriptures dealing with this question -

People I've spoken to about this question -

Here are some practical steps in seeking answers:

1. Pray that you will trust God, even when you don't understand.
2. Pray for wisdom.
3. Search Scripture. (Most Bibles have a concordance in the back where you can look up key words or themes; this is a great place to start.)
4. Ask your youth leader, pastor, family member(s), and/or trusted friends for prayer, Scripture, and insight from their own experiences.

Exodus 31:3	"And I have filled him with the Spirit of God, with skill, ability and knowedge in all kinds of crafts."
Deuteronomy 34:9	"Now Joshua son of Nun was filled with the spirit of wisdom because Moses had laid his hands on him. So the Israelites listened to him and did what the LORD had commanded Moses."
Micah 3:8	"But as for me, I am filled with power, with the Spirit of the LORD, and with justice and might, to declare to Jacob his transgression, to Israel his sin."
Luke 1:41	"When Elizabeth heard Mary's greeting, the baby leaped in her womb, and Elizabeth was filled with the Holy Spirit."
LUKE 1:67	"HIS FATHER ZECHARIAH WAS FILLED WITH THE HOLY SPIRIT AND PROPHESIED."
Luke 12:12	"For the Holy Spirit will teach you at that time what you should say."
John 20:22	"And with that he breathed on them and said, 'Receive the Holy Spirit.'"
ACTS 4:31	"AFTER THEY PRAYED, THE PLACE WHERE THEY WERE MEETING WAS SHAKEN. AND THEY WERE ALL FILLED WITH THE HOLY SPIRIT AND SPOKE THE WORD OF GOD BOLDLY."
Acts 5:32	"We are witnesses of these things, and so is the Holy Spirit, whom God has given to those who obey him."
Acts 11:24	"He was a good man, full of the Holy Spirit and faith, and a great number of people were brought to the Lord."
Romans 15:13	"May the God of hope fill you with all joy and peace as you trust in him, so that you may overflow with hope by the power of the Holy Spirit."
1 Corinthians 12:3	"Therefore I tell you that no one who is speaking by the Spirit of God says, Jesus be cursed,' and no one can say, 'Jesus is Lord,' except by the Holy Spirit."
Ephesians 5:18	"Do not get drunk on wine, which leads to debauchery. Instead, be filled with the Spirit."
1THESSALONIANS 4:8	"THEREFORE, HE WHO REJECTS THIS INSTRUCTION DOES NOT REJECT MAN BUT GOD, WHO GIVES YOU HIS HOLY SPIRIT."
Jude 20	"But you, dear friends, build yourselves up in your most holy faith and pray in the Holy Spirit."

IN TIME

Life in the Spirit is about being in tune with God. It is about learning to hear Him, trust Him, and follow Him. God has poured out His Spirit on us, so that we may know Him and make Him known. Simply put, this incredible gift empowers us to see what God is doing and join Him in His work.

In the story you're going to read, Jesus is just over a month old. His parents have brought him to the Temple to present sacrifices after the birth of their first child. The priest was a man named Simeon. He is an incredible picture of someone who trusted God, waiting patiently, without knowing all of the answers. Read Luke 2:25–32.

Here, Simeon is described in three different ways in relation to the Spirit: the Sprit was upon him, He revealed things to him, and He moved him. Verse 25 deals with Simeon's identity. Verse 26 deals with what he knew. Verse 27 deals with what he did.

Life in the Spirit requires total devotion. God has given Himself to us. We have to give ourselves to Him. Verse 25 shows us that Simeon was a righteous man, devoted to serving God, and eagerly anticipating the Messiah. His whole life was set apart as holy. He was looking for Christ every day. How committed are you to seeing the work of God daily? How would people describe your character?

Maybe the Spirit hasn't revealed something as specific to you as He did to Simeon in verse 26, but what has He revealed to you? What promises give you confidence?

Simeon followed the direction of the Spirit in verse 27 and he was able to see the Savior, just as God had promised. Are you in tune with God's Spirit? What are you doing to stay in a position to hear Him and sense His presence?

Finally, Simeon experienced peace and fulfillment because He trusted the Spirit. God keeps His promises. When the Spirit is upon you and moving, you can't help but praise God. Read Simeon's praise in verses 29–32, and then write a prayer expressing your own praise.

"The wind blows wherever it pleases. You hear its sound, but you cannot tell where it comes from or where it is going. So it is with everyone born of the Spirit." — John 3:8

CRUX

WHEN YOU HEAR PEOPLE SAY THE PHRASE, "THE GOSPEL," DOES IT SOUND OLD SCHOOL TO YOU? DON'T BE FOOLED. THE GOSPEL IS THE HEART OF GOD'S PLAN FOR REDEEMING HIS PEOPLE. THE GOSPEL IS THE STORY OF JESUS AND ALL HE DID TO PROVIDE A WAY FOR US, HIS CHILDREN, TO BE WITH HIM FOREVER. THE GOSPEL IS NOT IRRELEVANT, OUT-OF-DATE, OR UN-COOL. IT IS TIMELIER TODAY THAN EVER.

If you're looking for how the power of the gospel works in the world and in the lives of individual believers, the Book of Romans is the place to go. Paul's letter to the Christians in Rome spells out the availability of the gospel to all people, unpacks the implications of sin and the rewards of salvation, and calls all believers to be active in joining with God's mission to redeem the world. Think the gospel isn't relevant enough for today's world? Keep reading. You're about to be proven wrong.

SESSION 1 SOMETHING FOR EVERYONE — **PG 202-207**

SESSION 2 EVERYONE BLOWS IT — **PG 208-213**

SESSION 3 IN THE NICK OF TIME — **PG 214-219**

SESSION 4 GETTING THE WORD OUT — **PG 220-225**

SESSION 5 THE GOOD LIFE — **PG 226-231**

SESSION 6 CAUSE AND EFFECT — **PG 232-237**

THE GOSPEL IS POWER. WHAT IS THE GOSPEL? SIMPLY, IT IS THE LIFE SAVING STORY OF JESUS. THE GOSPEL IS THE STORY OF HOW GOD BECAME MAN, LIVED & TAUGHT AMONG HIS PEOPLE, ALLOWED HIMSELF TO BE SACRIFICED FOR THEIR SINS, & AROSE TO CLAIM VICTORY OVER SIN. THE GOSPEL IS SALVATION. IT HAS THE POWER TO SAVE ALL HUMANKIND FROM THEIR SINS. THE GOSPEL IS LIFE. THE GOSPEL IS POWER.

THE GOSPEL IS LOVE.

DEVOTION

What if you woke up one morning to find an epidemic is sweeping over your community. Some sort of killer virus is infecting people, so they would only have a few days to live. The community is in chaos. People are scared to go outside. Fear has set in. People are hysterical. No one knows what to do. But here's the catch: You are the only one who has the cure. Somehow, someway, you hold the antidote that will completely heal people of the disease. How cool is that?

What would you do? Well, it's obvious right? You'd keep quiet! No need in causing a fuss. I mean, what if someone didn't want to be healed? And how would you get the antidote to them? You wouldn't want to go knock on their door. After all, they might be eating dinner. And what if they didn't believe you? What then? See, you're better off keeping the antidote to yourself, right? Right . . .

Read Romans 1:14–17. Romans is a cool book; it is actually a letter written by Paul to the Christians in Rome. Paul wanted to visit the Christians there, to teach them and encourage them. So, before he came to visit, he sent them a letter. The Book of Romans is one of the most amazing books of the Bible. It contains an incredible summary of Paul's theology. In just a few chapters, Paul explained in amazing detail the power and importance of the gospel. It is a book no Christ-follower can afford to pass over.

In the passage you just read, Paul explained to his readers that nothing could make him keep the power of the gospel to himself. Paul understood that the story of Jesus is life to those who hear and believe. He wasn't about to keep it to himself.

Keeping the story of Jesus to ourselves is like keeping a life-saving antidote away from dying, diseased people. You wouldn't keep medicine from a sick person. Why do you hesitate to tell people about Jesus?

God's salvation is available to all people. But they must be told in order to believe. What are you waiting for?

T-SHIRT SUMMER
CAMP ATONEMENT
BRACELET JESUS
DISCIPLE NOW
RETREAT YOUTH
CHOIR SALVATION
SUNDAY SCHOOL
FCA CHURCH
FACEBOOK GROUP
BUMPER STICK-
ER GRACE LOCK-
INS WEDNESDAY
NIGHTS SACRIFICE
PRAISE MUSIC
SMALL GROUP
UNCONDITIONAL
LOVE MISSION
TRIP CONFERENCE

WHAT THE BIBLE SAYS
ABOUT THE GOSPEL

THE BEGINNING OF THE GOSPEL ABOUT JESUS CHRIST, THE SON OF GOD. MARK 1:1

IT HAS ALWAYS BEEN MY AMBITION TO PREACH THE GOSPEL WHERE CHRIST WAS NOT KNOWN. ROMANS 15:20

PRAY ALSO FOR ME, THAT WHENEVER I OPEN MY MOUTH, WORDS MAY BE GIVEN ME SO THAT I WILL FEARLESSLY MAKE KNOWN THE MYSTERY OF THE GOSPEL. EPHESIANS 6:19

AND THE GOSPEL MUST FIRST BE PREACHED TO ALL NATIONS. MARK 13:10

AND YOU ALSO WERE INCLUDED IN CHRIST WHEN YOU HEARD THE WORD OF TRUTH, THE GOSPEL OF YOUR SALVATION. EPHESIANS 1:13

I WANT YOU TO KNOW, BROTHERS, THAT THE GOSPEL I PREACHED IS NOT SOMETHING THAT MAN MADE UP. GALATIANS 1:11

YET WHEN I PREACH THE GOSPEL, I CANNOT BOAST, FOR I AM COMPELLED TO PREACH. WOE TO ME IF I DO NOT PREACH THE GOSPEL! I CORINTHIANS 9:16

ALL OVER THE WORLD THIS GOSPEL IS BEARING FRUIT AND GROWING, JUST AS IT HAS BEEN DOING AMONG YOU SINCE THE DAY YOU HEARD IT AND UNDERSTOOD GOD'S GRACE IN ALL ITS TRUTH. COLOSSIANS 1:6

WHATEVER HAPPENS, CONDUCT YOURSELVES IN A MANNER WORTHY OF THE GOSPEL OF CHRIST. PHILIPPIANS 1:27

HE WILL PUNISH THOSE WHO DO NOT KNOW GOD AND DO NOT OBEY THE GOSPEL OF OUR LORD JESUS. 2 THESSALONIANS 1:8

AND THIS GOSPEL OF THE KINGDOM WILL BE PREACHED IN THE WHOLE WORLD AS A TESTIMONY TO ALL NATIONS, AND THEN THE END WILL COME. MATTHEW 24:14

REMEMBER JESUS CHRIST, RAISED FROM THE DEAD, DESCENDED FROM DAVID. THIS IS MY GOSPEL. 2 TIMOTHY 2:8

THEN I SAW ANOTHER ANGEL FLYING IN MIDAIR, AND HE HAD THE ETERNAL GOSPEL TO PROCLAIM TO THOSE WHO LIVE ON THE EARTH—TO EVERY NATION, TRIBE, LANGUAGE AND PEOPLE.— REVELATION 14:6

GOSPEL FOR EVERYONE

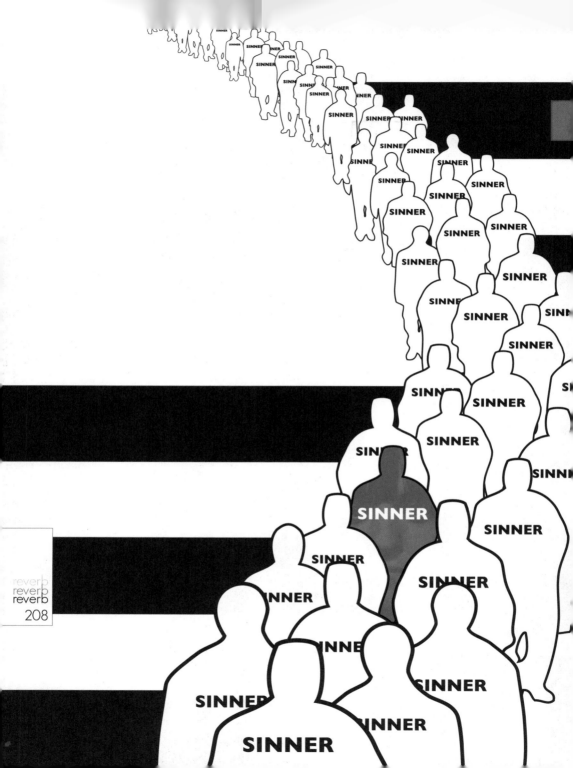

WHAT IS SIN?

SOME WORDS HAVE LOST THEIR MEANING. SIN SEEMS TO BE ONE OF THEM. WHEN YOU HEAR THE WORD SIN, DOES IT HAVE AN IMPACT ON YOU? DOES IT PAINT AN ACCURATE PICTURE OF REBELLION AGAINST GOD? WHEN YOU HEAR THAT JESUS SAVED YOU FROM YOUR SINS, YOU SHOULD BE ABLE TO IMMEDIATELY VISUALIZE HOW HORRIBLE SIN IS. STILL NEED HELP?

SO THAT YOU DO NOT FORGET WHAT SIN IS, HERE ARE A FEW WORDS TO JAR YOUR MEMORY. . .

ANIMOSITY, ENMITY, FURY, HATRED, ▪ IMPATIENCE, RAGE, ANNOYANCE, ▪ TEMPER, ▪ VIOLENCE GOSSIP, ADDICTION, DISHONESTY IMPURE THOUGHTS, ▪ RESENTMENT, ENVY, DENYING GOD, COVETOUSNESS, HOLDING A GRUDGE LYING TO YOUR FRIENDS, PRIDE DISOBEDIENCE, ▪ INDISCIPLINE GUILT, APATHY, INSUBORDINATION, LYING TO YOUR PARENTS REBELLION, BLOWING UP, STUBBORNNESS, BREAKING THE LAW INFURIATION, ▪ IMPURE LANGUAGE, ▪ FALLING SHORT, DEFIANCE, HYPOCRISY, UNRULINESS HATE, INDIGNATION, GLUTTONY DISLIKING SOMEONE, SEXUAL IMMORALITY, DECEITFULNESS, LUST UNGODLINESS, ▪ UNRIGHTEOUSNESS, ▪ JUDGMENTAL, ▪ WICKEDNESS, CHEATING, COMMITTING A CRIME, EVIL-DOING, ANGER, GOING AGAINST GOD'S DESIRES, STEALING, USING HATEFUL WORDS PUTTING SELF BEFORE OTHERS TURNING FROM GOD, SEXUAL IMPURITY, NO SELF CONTROL ▪

THERE'S HOPE

THESE ARE ALL TRUE STORIES OF TEENAGERS WHO USED BAD JUDGMENT, WERE OUTRIGHT WRONG, OR SIMPLY FAILED TO REFLECT CHRIST.

When I was 15, I was sitting with my girlfriend in church. I spotted another girl who I knew liked me. I began to do subtle things like put my arm around my girlfriend, or hold her hand... giving a slight wave to the other girl each time. Then I noticed that my girlfriend's father was sitting in the balcony. —TRAVIS

When I was 16 I fell asleep at the wheel, hit the side of a truck in oncoming traffic, and didn't stop. A bicycle cop stopped me at the next stop sign. While trying to pull over I knocked the cop off his bike. I was handcuffed and had to wait until my dad got to the scene. I walked away with only a "failure to maintain one lane of traffic" ticket. —BRIAN

The week before we played our big rival in football, a few of us seniors decided to go to the other team's practice and try and rattle them a bit. Within minutes of our arrival, someone called the cops. And even though I left at the first warning, one of my teammate's parents blamed the entire thing on me. On top of that, we lost the football game. —JASON

During my senior year, one of my best friends spent most of the weekends all through high school staying at my house. We were like sisters. But my friend got raped and ended up conceiving a child. She went to a home for unwed mothers. She asked me not to tell my mother about the pregnancy; she didn't want my mom to think less of her. I never told my mom and would often sneak excuses to go see my friend at the home. Her family wasn't embarrassed about the situation and threw her a baby shower. They sent an invitation to my mother! I had never been so dishonest with my parents before. My mom was devastated that I didn't tell her—ANONYMOUS

I was 13 years old, and it was the fourth of July. My parents wouldn't let me go outside and shoot fireworks. So I decided to shoot one in our den. I burnt my baby sister's leg and caught the carpet on fire. —LES

I was 15 when my girlfriend broke up with me. The next Wednesday night at church, I saw her and one of my best friends together. Long story short, he and I got in a fight outside. We had a visitor at youth group that night who had resisted coming to church because he felt Christians were hypocrites. I know I ruined an opportunity to reflect Christ.—JASON

When I was 13 I made fun of a disabled person in the presence of my unchurched friend. He told me he would never want to adhere to any religion I followed. —ERIN

When I was a sophomore I told a senior that I knew how to drive a stick shift just so I could drive across the street to the game. (I had no idea what a stick shift was.) I managed to stall out a few times, back into a telephone pole, and make the entire band late for a game. The senior never spoke to me again. —AMY

When I was in middle school several of my friends and I played a prank on our next-door neighbor's car. It ended up costing him $500 for repairs. He had to take the bus for months. I won't ever forget the guilt and regret I felt when I realized what I'd done to this poor stranger. —ALISON

ALL OF THESE PEOPLE ARE NOW IN THEIR 20'S AND 30'S. ALL OF THEM ARE SOLD-OUT FOLLOWERS OF CHRIST. MAKING A MISTAKE DOESN'T MEAN IT'S THE END OF YOUR RELATIONSHIP WITH GOD. GOD IS FAITHFUL AND WILL SEE YOU THROUGH. DON'T GIVE UP.

SIN IS SO SERIOUS THAT THE BIBLE USES A VARIETY OF WORDS TO DESCRIBE AND DEFINE IT. THERE ARE FOUR MAIN HEBREW ROOT WORDS FOR SIN. THE WORDS REFER TO MISSING THE MARK, REBELLING AGAINST GOD, DELIBERATELY TWISTING GOD'S COMMANDS, AND EVEN SINNING OUT OF IGNORANCE. THERE ARE ALSO MULTIPLE GREEK WORDS USED TO DESCRIBE SIN. THESE WORDS HAVE SIMILAR MEANINGS TO THE HEBREW WORDS. HOWEVER YOU LOOK AT IT, SIN IS THE IDEA OF GOING AGAINST GOD.

YOU KNOW WHAT SIN IS. BUT WHAT DOES SIN DO? SIN WILL CAUSE YOU TO LOSE FRIENDS. SIN WILL CAUSE YOU TO LOSE PEOPLE'S TRUST. SIN WILL CAUSE YOU TO LOSE YOUR GOOD REPUTATION. SIN WILL CAUSE YOU TO LOSE YOUR SELF-RESPECT. SIN WILL CAUSE YOU TO FEEL EMBARRASSMENT, GUILT, SHAME, PAIN, GRIEF, AND DOUBT. MOST OF ALL, SIN WILL PUT SPACE BETWEEN YOU AND GOD. YOU CANNOT DWELL IN GOD'S PRESENCE WHILE LIVING IN SIN. PUT SINFUL WAYS BEHIND YOU. TURN FROM ANY HABIT OF SIN IN YOUR LIFE.

EVERYBODY MAKES

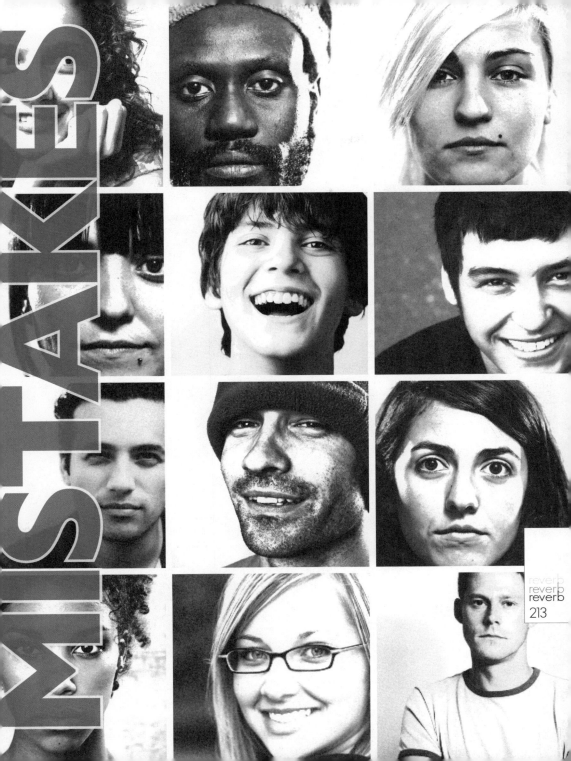

MISTAKES

WHAT MUST IT HAVE BEEN LIKE TO WATCH YOUR SON DIE? WE CAN ONLY IMAGINE THE PAIN. GOD ALLOWED JESUS TO BE PUNISHED FOR THE SINS OF ALL HUMANITY. MORE THAN THAT, GOD POURED OUT HIS WRATH AND JUDGMENT ON CHRIST. GOD THE FATHER TURNED HIS BACK ON GOD THE SON. WHAT DID JESUS DO TO DESERVE THIS? PRECIOUS JESUS. THE LORD OF LORDS. THE LAMB OF GOD. OUR SIN BROUGHT JESUS TO THIS MOMENT. YOUR SIN. BUT HE WILLINGLY TOOK THIS PATH FOR YOU. IT WASN'T A SURPRISE. JESUS WANTED TO PAY THIS SACRIFICE. HE WANTED TO SAVE YOU. AND MAKE NO MISTAKE. YOU WERE SAVED THROUGH HIS DEATH. BELIEVE IN HIM AND LIVE.

DEVOTION

How could you possibly deserve God's salvation?

After all, you don't bring a whole lot to the table.

God's moral standards are pretty high . . . as in, perfection. Pretty sure you don't live up to those.

God expects to be first in your life. Nothing else should come before Him. You probably don't always keep your end of the bargain there, either.

God created you to live for Him, to testify to the world about His greatness through your words and actions. Hmmm . . . Your words and actions don't always line up with God's plan, do they?

So how can you possibly be saved from the consequences of your sins? How can you expect to experience a life in heaven after this life on earth has ended?

Stop for a second and read Romans 5:6–10. You don't get very far before you come face to face with an amazing truth. When Christ died for you, He knew you were ungodly. He had no illusions. He did not think you would to be perfect only to get disappointed once He finally got to know you. He knew you had nothing to offer. That's what verse 6 means when it says you were powerless. Verse 8 says that God knew you were a sinner when He allowed His precious, only Son to be murdered in your place. Yet, God loved you so much that it was worth the price to Him.

It's true. There is nothing you can ever do to justify the gift God gave you. God doesn't ask you to justify it. He doesn't expect you to be able to make it worth His while. You never will. What does God expect?

God expects you to believe in and love Him. He expects you to stop living for you and to start living for Him. He expects you to help others see that this amazing gift is for them, too. And He expects you to continuously turn back to Him when you do goof up. And considering all Christ gave up for you, this doesn't seem like too much for God to expect from you.

GUESS THE PRICE

FORGIVENESS OF MY SINS

JESUS' LIFE

You're a teenager, so you're busy. When did you last take time to stop everything and praise God in prayer? You're about to get the opportunity to spend a few minutes in relationship with your Lord.

GUIDED
PRAYER

FOLLOW THE PROMPTS BELOW TO SPEND SOME TIME IN A GUIDED PRAYER WITH GOD. IF YOU CHOOSE, WRITE YOUR PRAYERS IN THE SPACE BELOW EACH PROMPT.

TAKE A MINUTE TO SIMPLY CONFESS YOUR SINFULNESS TO GOD. CONFESS SPECIFIC SINS IF YOU NEED TO, BUT MAINLY FOCUS ON YOUR SINFUL NATURE. CONFESS TO GOD THAT IF LEFT TO YOUR OWN DESIRES, YOU WOULD PUT YOURSELF ABOVE EVERYONE AND EVERYTHING. WRITE YOUR PRAYER IF YOU WANT.

NOW, THANK GOD FOR LOVING YOU ENOUGH TO HAVE A PLAN IN PLACE TO PAY YOUR SIN-DEBT. YOU COULDN'T HAVE A RELATION-SHIP WITH GOD UNLESS HE PROVIDED A WAY. THANK HIM FOR HIS WISDOM, POWER, AND LOVE. WRITE YOUR PRAYER IF YOU WANT.

FINALLY, THANK JESUS FOR WILLINGLY ENDURING THE PAIN AND SHAME OF YOUR SINS. PRAISE HIM FOR HIS UNENDING LOVE FOR YOU. TELL HIM HOW MUCH YOU LOVE HIM AND HOW YOU LONG TO FOLLOW HIM. WRITE YOUR PRAYER IF YOU WANT.

ROMANS 10:14 **HOW, THEN, CAN THEY CALL ON THE ONE THEY HAVE NOT BELIEVED IN? AND HOW CAN THEY BELIEVE IN THE ONE OF WHOM THEY HAVE NOT HEARD? AND HOW CAN THEY HEAR WITHOUT SOME-ONE PREACHING TO THEM? AND HOW CAN THEY PREACH UNLESS THEY ARE SENT? AS IT IS WRITTEN, "HOW BEAUTIFUL ARE THE FEET OF THOSE WHO BRING GOOD NEWS!"**

GET COMFORTABLE DESCRIBING YOUR LIFE BEFORE YOU SUBMITTED YOUR WILL TO JESUS. IN THE SPACE BELOW, TAKE FIVE SENTENCES TO TALK ABOUT HOW YOU VIEWED YOUR LIFE BEFORE YOU BECAME A CHRIST-FOLLOWER.

NOW, EXPLAIN THE NEED

There had to be something that led you to believe that you were a sinner in need of saving. Explain how you knew that submitting your life to Christ was the way to purpose, life, joy, and salvation. In three to five sentences, write how you came to understand the need to give your life to Christ. Work in the following verses somewhere in your story:

Romans 3:23 "For all have sinned and fall short of the glory of God."
Romans 6:23 "For the wages of sin is death, but the gift of God is eternal life in Christ Jesus our Lord."

BRING IN THE WORD

Because the Bible is God's Word, you'll want to know how to lead someone through some Scriptures that help them understand Christ's role in salvation. Memorize the following verses and use them to help someone see that Christ is the way to life.

Romans 5:8 "But God demonstrates his own love for us in this: While we were still sinners, Christ died for us."
John 14:6 "Jesus answered, 'I am the way and the truth and the life. No one comes to the Father except through me.'"

WRAP IT UP

Now, take three sentences to talk about how your life is different now that you serve Jesus.

PRACTICE DELIVERING THIS STORY. WHEN THE TIME COMES, THE HOLY SPIRIT WILL USE YOUR STORY TO HELP LEAD SOMEONE TO GIVING THEIR LIFE TO CHRIST.

WHAT IF?

WHAT IF YOU HAD A MAGIC BOX THAT CONTAINED
AN UNLIMITED SUPPLY OF MONEY?

I mean it ... truly unlimited. Every time you reached in your hand to pull out a stack of bills, a new stack took its place. This would give you unlimited pleasure, right? But wouldn't you want to share? Think about what you could do for your family, your friends ... even strangers. Then think about how you could change the world. You would have the power to dramatically impact people's lives for the better.

The life-changing story of Jesus is the same way. You have it in you... Give it away! If you really believe it, how can you keep it to yourself?

CAN i BE SAVED?

UH OH!

THINK YOU HAVE WHAT IT TAKES? OR WORRIED YOU MIGHT NOT ADD UP? TAKE THIS QUIZ! FIND OUT IF YOU HAVE THE GOODS TO BE A CANDIDATE FOR THE SALVATION JESUS WON ON THE CROSS FOR ALL HUMANKIND.

When you've finished the quiz, add the numbers from each of your answers and compare them to the answers found in the Key.

FIND OUT IF YOU'RE GOOD ENOUGH TO BE SAVED!

How often do you use cuss words?
5 POINTS: Less than once a month
3 POINTS: Three to five times a month
I POINT: Once or twice a week
-3 POINTS: Daily

How many times have you lied to your parents in your life?
5 POINTS: Count the number on two hands
3 POINTS: Need your feet to count
I POINT: Need to borrow your friend's hands to count
-3 POINTS: Will need hands and feet of entire marching band

Have you ever broken the law?
5 POINTS: Never
3 POINTS: Only occasionally
I POINT: More than I'd like to admit
-3 POINTS: The police know me by first name

Would you ever talk about your best friend behind his or her back?
5 POINTS: Absolutely not
3 POINTS: Try really hard not to
I POINT: Occasionally
-3 POINTS: Oops! Talked about them today

Do you ever put your own needs before the needs of others?
5 POINTS: No
3 POINTS: Maybe
I POINTS: Yes, occasionally
-3 POINTS: All the time

What is your attitude towards the poor, the sick, and the social outcasts?
5 POINTS: Seek to love and serve them
3 POINTS: Help when I can
I POINTS: Know that I am supposed to help
-3 POINTS: They are a nuisance

If you were taking a test and your teacher left the answer key where you could see it, would you be tempted to cheat?
5 POINTS: Definitely not
3 POINTS: Tempted, wouldn't cheat
I POINTS: Might cheat
-3 POINTS: Would definitely take advantage

ADD UP YOUR SCORE AND SEE IF YOU ARE SAVE-ABLE!
35-29 SWEET! DEFINITELY SAVE-ABLE
28-22 OH, YEAH! YOU'RE SAVE-ABLE
21-15 HAVE NO FEAR! YOU'RE SAVE-ABLE

ALL CALL WHO WORSHIP CHRIST YOU

WILL BE DISPLAYED

LOVE MUST BE SINCERE

HATE WHAT IS EVIL

CLING TO WHAT IS GOOD

LIVE AT PEACE WITH EVERYONE

DEVOTION

James Frey had an amazing story. And it was immediately obvious that people wanted to hear him tell it. Frey's bestselling book, A Million Little Pieces, is a chilling account of a life of drug addiction and harmful behavior. Frey painted a picture that was painfully honest, with graphic details of the sinister life he lived while addicted to drugs. Oprah invited him on her show and featured his book in her book club. People all over America were captivated.

There was one problem, though. Frey had made up most of the story. He had lied about or otherwise exaggerated many of the accounts in the book.

Read Romans 12:9–21. Paul said a lot here. He basically summed up what it means to live a life of Christian character. He outlined many ways humanity can live according to God's standards. But maybe the line that serves as the best summary of the passage is in verse 9: "Hate what is evil; cling to what is good."

If we are to follow Christ, we must hate what is evil. We must live a life that clings to the good things of God. Why? First of all, Christ commanded us to live this way. All of Scripture attests to the fact that God is holy, righteous, and just. As His children, our lives should mirror His character.

But the other reason we should live good lives is because our lives are our most powerful testimony to the world. The world hates a fake. James Frey is a perfect example. His fans turned on him when they found out his stories were embellished. Those we are trying to influence for Christ will turn on us if our actions do not match our professed beliefs. If you say you are a Christ-follower, you must be prepared to live a life that testifies to God's greatness.

The worst thing you can do is to communicate to the world that following Christ doesn't change your life. If you live like the rest of the world, you show people that Jesus isn't important enough to make a difference. You say to the world that there is no rush to turn your life over to Christ.

Don't send the wrong message! Live a right life for Christ . . . today!

The passage below is from the twelfth chapter of Paul's letter to the Romans. It is a cool passage in that it is kind of like a list. It's ike Paul is saying, "Do this, and this, and this . . ."

Read the passage on the left. Then, in the space provided on the right, for each verse listed, write how you can practically live out Paul's instructions in today's world. Then, think of this list as your "to do" list for living a Christ-like life today.

Rom. 12:9 Love must be sincere. Hate what is evil; cling to what is good.

Rom. 12:10 Be devoted to one another in brotherly love. Honor one another above yourselves.

Rom. 12:11 Never be lacking in zeal, but keep your spiritual fervor, serving the Lord.

Rom. 12:12 Be joyful in hope, patient in affliction, faithful in prayer.

Rom. 12:13 Share with God's people who are in need. Practice hospitality.

Rom. 12:14 Bless those who persecute you; bless and do not curse.

Rom. 12:15 Rejoice with those who rejoice; mourn with those who mourn.

Rom. 12:16 Live in harmony with one another. Do not be proud, but be willing to associate with people of low position. Do not be conceited.

Rom. 12:17 Do not repay anyone evil for evil. Be careful to do what is right in the eyes of everybody.

Rom. 12:18 If it is possible, as far as it depends on you, live at peace with everyone.

TO DO:

HYPOCRITE

The word comes from the Greek word *hypokritēs*, which means "actor."

WEBSTER'S GIVES TWO DEFINITIONS FOR THE WORD HYPOCRITE: 1. "A PERSON WHO ACTS IN CONTRADICTION TO HIS OR HER STATED BELIEFS OR FEELINGS"; 2. "A PERSON WHO PUTS ON A FALSE APPEARANCE OF VIRTUE OR RELIGION."

JESUS HAD A FEW THINGS TO SAY ABOUT HYPOCRITES, AS WELL.

MATTHEW 23:27 "WOE TO YOU, TEACHERS OF THE LAW AND PHARISEES, YOU HYPOCRITES! YOU ARE LIKE WHITEWASHED TOMBS, WHICH LOOK BEAUTIFUL ON THE OUTSIDE BUT ON THE INSIDE ARE FULL OF DEAD MEN'S BONES AND EVERYTHING UNCLEAN.

MATTHEW 6:2 "SO WHEN YOU GIVE TO THE NEEDY, DO NOT ANNOUNCE IT WITH TRUMPETS, AS THE HYPOCRITES DO IN THE SYNAGOGUES AND ON THE STREETS, TO BE HONORED BY MEN. I TELL YOU THE TRUTH, THEY HAVE RECEIVED THEIR REWARD IN FULL.

MATTHEW 23:23 "WOE TO YOU, TEACHERS OF THE LAW AND PHARISEES, YOU HYPOCRITES! YOU GIVE A TENTH OF YOUR SPICES—MINT, DILL AND CUMMIN. BUT YOU HAVE NEGLECTED THE MORE IMPORTANT MATTERS OF THE LAW—JUSTICE, MERCY AND FAITHFULNESS. YOU SHOULD HAVE PRACTICED THE LATTER, WITHOUT NEGLECTING THE FORMER.

MATTHEW 6:5 "AND WHEN YOU PRAY, DO NOT BE LIKE THE HYPOCRITES, FOR THEY LOVE TO PRAY STANDING IN THE SYNAGOGUES AND ON THE STREET CORNERS TO BE SEEN BY MEN.

MARK 7:6 HE REPLIED, "ISAIAH WAS RIGHT WHEN HE PROPHESIED ABOUT YOU HYPOCRITES; AS IT IS WRITTEN: "'THESE PEOPLE HONOR ME WITH THEIR LIPS, BUT THEIR HEARTS ARE FAR FROM ME.'"

MATTHEW 6:16 "WHEN YOU FAST, DO NOT LOOK SOMBER AS THE HYPOCRITES DO, FOR THEY DISFIGURE THEIR FACES TO SHOW MEN THEY ARE FASTING.

IF YOU ARE A FOLLOWER OF CHRIST, THERE IS NO ROOM IN YOUR LIFE FOR HYPOCRISY. IF YOU CLAIM TO BE A FOLLOWER, LIVE LIKE ONE. IT'S AS SIMPLE AS THAT.

LIVE HARMONY

ROMANS 15:5 MAY
THE GOD WHO GIVES
ENDURANCE AND
ENCOURAGEMENT
GIVE YOU A SPIRIT
OF UNITY AMONG
YOURSELVES AS YOU
FOLLOW CHRIST JESUS
SO THAT WITH ONE
HEART AND MOUTH
YOU MAY GLORIFY
THE GOD AND FATHER
OF OUR LORD
JESUS CHRIST.

DEVOTION

Take a moment and clear your mind of any distraction. Don't think about your responsibilities, or problems, or stressors . . . just relax for a second—for real.

Relaxed? Mind clear? Good . . .

Here's a statement to think about now that you're in the mood for thinking:

The life of a follower is hard.

Living as a Christ-follower in this world is not easy, is it? The more devoted you are to doing what God wants you to do, the harder it gets. It's easier to go with the crowd than it is to take a stand. How are you supposed to stay strong? How are you supposed to keep going in this world where it seems like everyone is against you?

As you might imagine, the Bible has a few things to say about this. Pause for a moment and read Romans 15:1–7. If you look closely, there are two verses in this passage that will help you out tremendously in living the life of a Christ-follower.

Verse 4 promises encouragement and confidence from reading God's Word. Now, don't take this lightly. The Bible is not like any other book. Hebrews 4:12 says that it is "living and active." Romans 15:4 alludes to this. Paul said that everything recorded in Scripture is written so that you might have hope and encouragement when things get tough. When life gets you down, turn to God's Word. This is one of the reasons He gave it to us.

The second promise for helping you out in this life is found in verse 5. Read it again. Here, God promises to give you encouragement, endurance, and a spirit of unity. So not only will God supernaturally give you His strength to stay strong and finish the race, but He also promises to surround you with fellow followers so you are not on this journey alone. How cool is that?

When life gets you down or when you are beaten up because you took a stand for Christ, turn to His Word and to your friends who share your faith. Doing both of these will not only help you on your journey, but you will also glorify God as the giver of good things. He is your Father and He loves to take care of His children. Give God a chance show you how good He is at it.

GOD

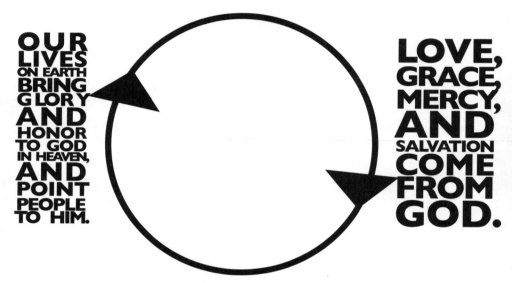

OUR LIVES ON EARTH BRING GLORY AND HONOR TO GOD IN HEAVEN, AND POINT PEOPLE TO HIM.

LOVE, GRACE, MERCY, AND SALVATION COME FROM GOD.

OUR LIVES ON EARTH ARE LIVED ACCORDING TO GOD'S COMMANDS.

HUMANKIND

NOT OK TO NOT GET ALONG

IS IT OK TO *NOT* LIKE SOME PEOPLE? YOUR FIRST ANSWER IS PROBABLY SOMETHING LIKE, "YES. AFTER ALL, YOU CAN'T GET ALONG WITH EVERYBODY." THIS MIGHT COME AS A SURPRISE TO YOU, BUT PAUL SEEMS TO THINK THAT MAYBE IT'S *NOT* OK TO *NOT* LIKE PEOPLE. CHECK IT OUT . . .

You've already read Romans 15:1-7. But go back and look at that last verse. Re-write verse 7 in your own words in the space below:

The cool thing about verse 7 is the reason Paul gives for why we should accept people. Paul doesn't say, "accept people because Christians are supposed to be all nice and what-not." Nope. Paul says something way more important and way more awesome.

Paul said in verse 7, "Accept one another, then, _____ _____ _____ _____ _____, in order to bring praise to God. (Fill in the blanks in the sentence above.)

Paul was trying to get us to understand that we have to be accepting of others because Christ first accepted us. And were we friends of God's when He accepted us? Absolutely not! In Romans 5:10 Paul wrote, "For if, when we were God's enemies, we were reconciled to him through the death of his Son, how much more, having been reconciled, shall we be saved through His life!" We were God's enemies due to the sin in our lives. But knowing that, God still sent Jesus for our sins.

If God accepted us when we were His enemies, aren't we supposed to accept those who are our enemies? If Jesus demonstrated the greatest act of love in all of history, giving His perfect life for us when we were His enemies, is it too much to ask for us to love someone we don't like?

The answer is that we must accept all people, love them in the name of Christ, and demonstrate to them the difference God makes in our lives. Why should we go the extra mile and do this? Look back at verse 7 one more time to find out.

At the end of verse 7 it tells us why we should accept others. What is the reason?

That's right . . . when we accept others, we bring praise to God. People see a difference in us. And if they look close enough, they realize the difference is not us, but God in us.

Don't you want to have that kind of impact on the world around you?

ANODTHUTHIHYO
AMORIEDLOU
GLORIFY C

Your life speaks. But what is it saying? Your words obviously matter, but so do your attitude and your actions. They scream something to the world around you . . . but what? Does your life testify to selfishness? Cowardice? Arrogance? Indulgence? Greed? Vanity? Compassion? Generosity? Freedom? Peace? Salvation? What?

All the little things: your quirks, your style, your strengths and weaknesses, they all add up to reveal one dominant voice in your life. Each little nuance to your personality and behavior is like a note in a steady crescendo, building toward this defining sound that will resonate deep in the lives of others around you. This booming declaration made with your life rattles in eternity. Everything matters. Are the chords your life strikes when interacting with others those of harmony? Is your song one of praise? Is your cry one of defeat or a resounding battle cry, defying the opposition of this world and rallying fellow rebels to join the revolution?

Are you going to limp and whimper along, or are you going to boldly pledge your allegiance to the Kingdom of God, devoting your life to His mission? Stand up or shut up.

SESSION 1 MOSES: SURRENDER TO THE MISSION—PG 240-245

SESSION 2 ELIJAH: ON MISSION IN A HOSTILE WORLD—PG 246-251

SESSION 3 JOHN THE BAPTIST: ON MISSION REGARDLESS OF COST—PG 252-257

SESSION 4 NEHEMIAH: RISING TO THE CHALLENGE—PG 258-263

SESSION 5 PHILIP: ANYTIME, ANYWHERE—PG 264-269

SESSION 6 BARNABAS: SUPPORTING AS WE GO—PG 270-275

WHO MADE YOUR MOUTH?

EX411

"Now go; I will help you speak
and will teach you what to say

EXODUS 4

hide or heed.

When God calls, how do you respond? There are really only two responses. Everything can ultimately be broken down into these basic categories: You can hide. Or you can heed.

Open your Bible to Genesis 3 and read verses 1-10. God created humanity to be in relationship with Him and with each other. Life was great until they started entertaining the idea that they should have the right to make their own decisions based on their own understanding. Immediately after their disobedience, sin infected their relationship with God. When God was walking in the garden, He called them, but they turned away and hid themselves.

If you're ignoring His call on your life, you're buying into the same lie as Adam and Eve. You naively think you can know what is best and most fulfilling for your life. Do you really think that you can ignore His voice or hide from Him? He knows who you are, where you are, and what you are doing, have done, and will do . . . because He created you, remember?

How are you hiding from God? What are you trying to hide from Him due to guilt or selfishness? (Don't try to make excuses or pass the blame like Adam and Eve did; be honest.)

Now turn to the first book of the New Testament. Read Matthew 4:17-25. Jesus came as what Paul refers to as the second Adam, meaning He is the new beginning for humanity's relationship with God. He called people to turn back to God (repent). When Christ was walking along, He called the disciples who immediately dropped everything and followed Him. Those heeding His call were healed. Instead of the knowledge of good and evil, their eyes were opened to the good news of life in God's Kingdom.

Whatever you've been hanging on to, drop it. Drop everything. Let God heal you and bring you back into a perfect and trusting relationship with Him. Just as He took fishermen and made them fishers of men, God is calling you to become part of His work. Stop hiding; heed His call today. Write a prayer below expressing your desire to turn away from sin and follow Him. Express your desire to be used by Him. How will you begin spreading the gospel and bring people to Jesus so that they too might be healed and transformed through a relationship with God?

MY PRAYER:

Genesis 22:11 "But the angel of the LORD called out to him from heaven, 'Abraham! Abraham!'
        'Here I am,' he replied."

here i am.

Genesis 46:2 "And God spoke to Israel in a vision at night and said, 'Jacob! Jacob!'
        'Here I am,' he replied."

Exodus 3:4 "When the LORD saw that he had gone over to look, God called to him from within the bush, 'Moses! Moses!'
        And Moses said, 'Here I am.'"

1 Samuel 3:4,10 "Then the LORD called Samuel.
        Samuel answered, 'Here I am.'
The LORD came and stood there, calling as at the other times, 'Samuel! Samuel!'
        Then Samuel said, 'Speak, for your servant is listening.'"

Isaiah 6:8 "Then I heard the voice of the Lord saying, 'Whom shall I send? And who will go for us?'
        And I said, 'Here am I, Send me!'"

Acts 9:10 "In Damascus there was a disciple named Ananias. The Lord called to him in a vision, 'Ananias!'
        'Yes, Lord,' he answered."

Romans 1:6 "And you also are among those who are called to belong to Jesus Christ."

(ARE YOU LISTENING? WHAT IS YOUR REPLY?)

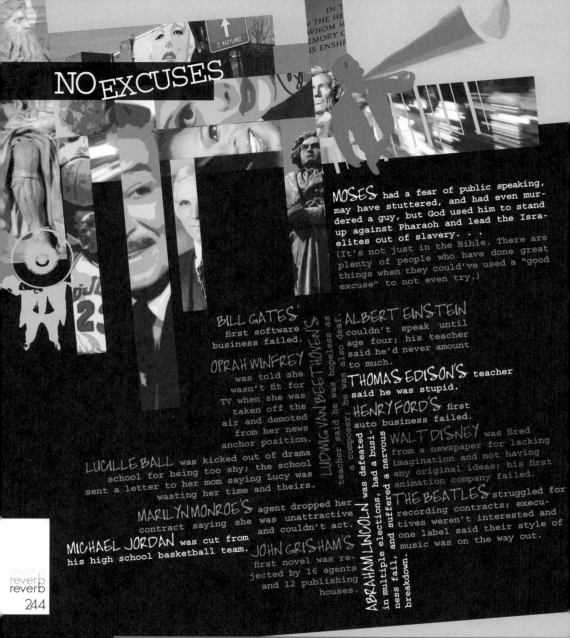

NO EXCUSES

MOSES had a fear of public speaking, may have stuttered, and had even murdered a guy, but God used him to stand up against Pharaoh and lead the Israelites out of slavery. . .
(It's not just in the Bible. There are plenty of people who have done great things when they could've used a "good excuse" to not even try.)

BILL GATES' first software business failed.

OPRAH WINFREY was told she wasn't fit for TV when she was taken off the air and demoted from her news anchor position.

LUCILLE BALL was kicked out of drama school for being too shy; the school sent a letter to her mom saying Lucy was wasting her time and theirs.

MARILYN MONROE'S agent dropped her contract saying she was unattractive and couldn't act.

MICHAEL JORDAN was cut from his high school basketball team.

JOHN GRISHAM'S first novel was rejected by 16 agents and 12 publishing houses.

LUDWIG VAN BEETHOVEN'S teacher said he was hopeless as a composer; he was also deaf.

ABRAHAM LINCOLN was defeated in multiple elections, had a business fail, and suffered a nervous breakdown.

ALBERT EINSTEIN couldn't speak until age four; his teacher said he'd never amount to much.

THOMAS EDISON'S teacher said he was stupid.

HENRY FORD'S first auto business failed.

WALT DISNEY was fired from a newspaper for lacking imagination and not having any original ideas; his first animation company failed.

THE BEATLES struggled for recording contracts; executives weren't interested and one label said their style of music was on the way out.

YOU. What's your excuse? Maybe you've blown it or have some phobia issue. Are you going to let anything keep you from pursuing God call on your life? He has great things in store for you.

Viral video. The mystery and intrigue of those two words is almost unbearable. Will it be hilarious, bizarre, amazing, or disgusting? Whatever it might be, something about a viral video draws your attention. You just have to look! After seeing it, you can't help but want to share it with everyone. It gets passed around from one person to the next. It's contagious.

Check out Exodus 3:1-14. Moses was in the middle of a normal day, doing shepherd stuff, when God sent Him an incredible message. Nobody had ever seen anything like this before; Moses couldn't help but look. (Now this may not sound impressive today with our technology and special effects, but stop for a second to think about the miracle of the burning bush.) The Israelites were suffering. God knew it. He drew Moses' attention and called him to take action.

Moses didn't feel worthy to be used by God, and he wasn't. Neither are we. But God is calling us to action as well. There are people all around you in bondage to sin, suffering from abuse, or crying out in exhaustion. The truth will set them free. What does God have to do to get your attention, so that you will listen and respond?

Two words: I AM. (That's how God identified Himself to Moses.) Unlike everything else, God doesn't change. He isn't some passing fad. God is mysterious. Life with Him should intrigue you. It's OK if it even scares you a little. But once you get a glimpse of God's mission, it becomes contagious. You can't wait to share Him with everyone else. So, spread the gospel today. God is aware of what's happening and He's asking you to step up, speak out, and do something about it!

"So DO NOT FEAR, for I am with you; do not be dismayed, for I am your God. I will strengthen you and help you; I will uphold you with my righteous right hand.

'All who rage against you will surely be ashamed and disgraced; those who oppose you will be as nothing and perish. Though you search for your enemies, you will not find them. Those who wage war against you will be as nothing at all. For I am the LORD, your God, who takes hold of your right hand and says to you, DO NOT FEAR; I will help you.'"
—Isaiah 41:10–13

"But now, this is what the LORD says—he who created you, O Jacob, he who formed you, O Israel:

'FEAR NOT, for I have redeemed you; I have summoned you by name; you are mine. When you pass through the waters, I will be with you; and when you pass through the rivers, they will not sweep over you. When you walk through the fire, you will not be burned; the flames will not set you ablaze. For I am the LORD, your God, the Holy One of Israel, your Savior.'"
—Isaiah 43:1–3

devotion.

Have you ever tried to hide from or avoid somebody? Maybe you went the long way around the school to avoid someone on a particular hallway. Maybe somebody is always picking at you . . . that annoying guy who likes to see how hard he can punch people or the girl who always has some biting comment. Maybe it's even a parent; you try to stay out of the house or in your room, keeping contact to a minimum. Something happened to create tension, and now it feels like a shadow, constantly lurking under your feet and around every corner. It's miserable.

Read 1 Kings 19:1-18. By taking a stand for God against Jezebel's false prophets, Elijah had become the focus of the queen's wrath. Here, Elijah was on the run and miserable. Repeatedly, he reminded God that he always tried to do the right thing and stood up for God's truth, but now he felt lonely and worn out. Nobody seemed to want anything to do with Elijah or God, so he started to withdraw. He tried to sleep away his rejection. He hid away in a cave. He felt as if he was the only one who cared.

But Elijah was not alone, and neither are you. God called him out of hiding. No, the world is not going to welcome you and your message with open arms. Actually, the world will resist and may even attack you and the gospel for which you live. But you can't just run away and hide. No matter what you feel like, God will not let anything overwhelm you. There are other believers out there, too.

NO.

NO.

NO.

what are you doing here? GO.

IKG. 19:11-13

you are not alone.

Sometimes, like Elijah, you may feel like the whole world has sold out and gone completely insane. It's pretty common to feel like you're the only one who cares. "Why even try?" You might think, "What difference will it make; I'm just one person." (But this is a lie from the Deceiver.) Like Elijah, sometimes God needs to remind us that we're not alone. . . .

YOUR ELISHA

Write down the name of that one spiritually mature person who could be your close friend to share in God's mission. Talk to this person and commit to praying for each other.

THE 7,000

Write down the name of as many Christ-followers as you can think of, even people you don't know but have heard about (both living and in history). Let this list serve as an encouragement to you.

Let's take a look at one of the most intense showdowns in biblical history. Elijah is having constant run-ins with the local king, Ahab, and his idolatrous queen, Jezebel. (For background on the conflict between God's prophet and the royal couple, read 1 Kings 16:30-17:1.)

What sins does the world around you dismiss as trivial? Not only in our culture, but also in your own youth group, what is ignored or considered no big deal even though God's Word clearly says it's wrong?

Now read 1 Kings 18:17-21. Elijah seemed seriously outnumbered; in fact, he felt alone. The prophet was labeled a troublemaker. He was an outsider, shunned to live on the fringes of his society. Confident in God's power, Elijah challenged the king (and the 450 prophets of Baal) to a duel of sorts. Read verses 22-35. Things were getting wild. The prophets of Baal tried to get the imaginary god's attention anyway possible, even cutting themselves, hoping the blood would provoke Baal into action. But you can't wake a deity that doesn't exist.

Elijah made sure that there could be no mistaking God's miraculous provision, by soaking the wood and offering with water. (The twelve stones and twelve pitchers symbolized the twelve tribes of Israel and God's work to reunite His community.) Elijah was confident in God's miraculous intercession, as God had taken care of Elijah's every need while he lived in the desert.

sacrifice.

How have you experienced God's provision/power? What confidence does this provide you for standing up against a hostile culture?

In verses 36-39, Elijah prays not for his own protection but for the truth of God to be clear to the enemies surrounding him. God answered that prayer, completely consuming the sacrifice. Not only did fire fall from heaven, but it also consumed the water, the dirt, and even the rocks of the altar! Now that was some serious heat.

Finally, keeping that in mind, turn to Romans 12 and read verses 1-2. Here, Paul said that we are now living proof of God's power and truth. We do not literally participate in sacrificial rituals anymore; Christ made that unnecessary. Yet, our lifestyle becomes our sacrifice. The Holy Spirit has come down like fire and completely consumed us. Like Elijah, we can have confidence of God's will for our lives when our hearts and minds are devoted to knowing His Word and responding to His voice. Have you completely surrendered everything in your life? Has God consumed every little area of your life as a living sacrifice? How will a wild world see the unmistakable power of God in your life?

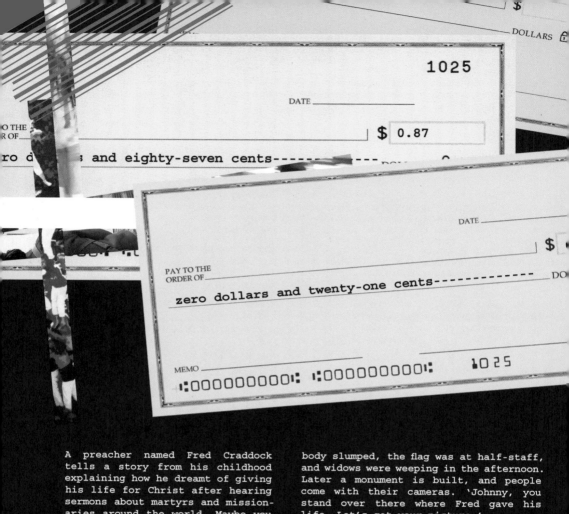

1025

DATE _____

$ 0.87

ro d...s and eighty-seven cents----------- ...

DATE _____

$ _____

PAY TO THE
ORDER OF _____

zero dollars and twenty-one cents------------- DO

MEMO _____

⑈000000000⑈ ⑈000000000⑈ 1025

A preacher named Fred Craddock tells a story from his childhood explaining how he dreamt of giving his life for Christ after hearing sermons about martyrs and missionaries around the world. Maybe you know how he feels. Maybe you've felt as if "real Christians" do huge things for God and you'll never be asked to sacrifice your life . . . but maybe you are giving your life, every day, in different ways.

Craddock remembers thinking, "It's a shame you can't be a Christian in this little town. Nobody is chasing or imprisoning or killing Christians.

"I pictured myself against a gray wall and some soldier saying, 'One last chance to deny Christ and live.' I confessed my faith, and they said 'Ready, aim, fire.' The

body slumped, the flag was at half-staff, and widows were weeping in the afternoon. Later a monument is built, and people come with their cameras. 'Johnny, you stand over there where Fred gave his life. Let's get your picture.'

"I was sincere then as I have been these forty-five years since. 'I give my life,' but nobody warned me that I could not write one big check. I've had to write forty-five years of little checks: 87 cents, 21 cents, a dollar three cents. Just nibbled away at this giving of life."

(Fred Craddock, Craddock Stories. St. Louis: Chalice Press, 2001, p. 155.)

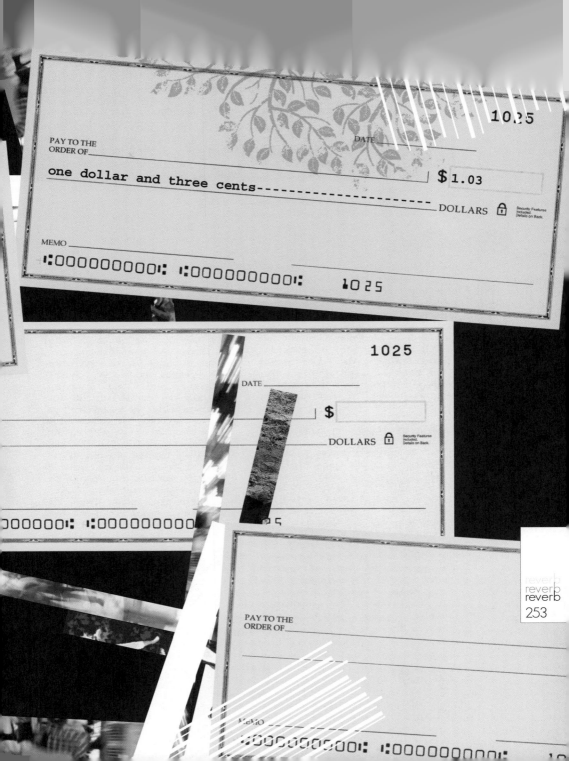

PAY TO THE
ORDER OF

DATE

1025

one dollar and three cents------------------------- $1.03

DOLLARS 🔒 Security Features Included. Details on Back.

MEMO

⑈000000000⑈ ⑈000000000⑈ 1025

1025

DATE

$

DOLLARS 🔒 Security Features Included. Details on Back.

000000⑈ ⑈000000000⑈

PAY TO THE
ORDER OF

MEMO

reverb
reverb
reverb
253

devotion.

First in line . . . everything in you wants to be first in line. You plan on camping out for days if necessary. Worse case scenario, plan-B means not even flinching at the chance to pay a scalper an outrageous price for a ticket. You have to be there. Missing out for any reason is simply not an option. Your mind even wanders to fantastic extremes of sneaking in, outrunning security, scaling walls . . . whatever it takes. No price is too great, no risk unreasonable; nothing will keep you from this experience of a lifetime. (Whatever your obsession: a sporting event, concert, premier, release—you name it.)

Grab your Bible and open it to Mark 6:17–29. Read about the price John the Baptist paid for refusing to compromise his message. John had seriously offended Herodias; well, enraged is more like it. Nobody likes having his or her sin called out and John never held any punches. As far as he was concerned, God's standard didn't play favorites, making exceptions for powerful or popular people. So when John called Herod out on his twisted little love triangle involving the wife of his brother, he stepped on toes that weren't used to getting stepped on.

It's no secret what happens when you cross the wrong girl. Pretty "Miss popular" ended up demanding John's head on a platter, and Herod delivered. Can't you just see that party?

It's easy for us to think we've got it so bad when others leave us out or make fun of us. Nobody will pretend like that doesn't hurt—it's real. And honestly, that may be the extent of what God is calling you to endure. But are you willing to stare down any suffering or rejection, and give up everything for the sake of God's Kingdom? No matter how great or seemingly insignificant the cost, are you willing to pay the price for following Christ? And there is a cost. Every day there is a price to pay. Like John, will you not even flinch, jumping at any opportunity to make any sacrifice in order to see God at work? Never compromise. God doesn't.

cut the cord.

THEY'LL THINK YOU'RE OUT OF YOUR MIND.
THEY'LL THINK YOU'VE LOST YOUR HEAD.
THEY'LL THINK YOU'VE GONE CRAZY.
THEY'LL THINK YOU'VE GIVEN UP TOO MUCH.
THEY'LL THINK YOU'RE TAKING IT TOO FAR.

Trust Him with everything.
Hold back nothing.
Be ready for anything.

GO AHEAD.
DIE TO YOURSELF.
LIVE FOR CHRIST.

CUT THE CORD.
GROW UP.
STEP OUT IN FAITH.

GOD'S TRUTH ISN'T A TRACK FOR PRIVATE LISTENING.
THE GOSPEL IS MEANT TO BE PLAYED OUT LOUD.
IT IS MEANT TO BE LIVED OUT LOUD.
FOR ALL TO HEAR.
IT IS MEANT TO BE GIVEN AWAY.
IT IS MEANT TO BE SHARED.
IT IS FREE.
BUT THERE IS A COST.

Nothing can silence it.
(So stop keeping it to yourself.)
Cut the cord and turn it up.
Live out loud.

on one hand,
but on the other...

WRITE DOWN EVERY
SACRIFICE or
PRICE
YOU HAVE PAID OR MAY EVER
NEED TO PAY FOR FOLLOWING
CHRIST.

WRITE DOWN EVERY
PROMISE
of GOD
AND REWARD OR BENEFIT FOR LIVING
LOUD, TESTIFYING THE GOSPEL
of CHRIST.

John the Baptist . . . this wasn't a denominational title. Technically, John was Jewish, and there was no such thing as denominations 2,000 years ago. He was known for his radical lifestyle, one that spoke at least as loud as the message he boldly preached. Baptism, for John, was a public declaration of surrender and identification with the Kingdom of God. It was a personal testimony of repentance and being cleansed from sin. If you were given a name or title, what would it be? For what are you known?

Read Luke 1:2-17. Before his parents even knew they would have a baby, God already knew what He would do through John's life. John would live radically different from the culture, even the religious culture. Knowing God has always had a purpose for your life as well, what things do you choose to abstain from in order to focus full attention on God? How does your attitude and lifestyle prepare people for the Lord?

Mark 1:6 tells us that "John wore clothing made of camel's hair, with a leather belt around his waist, and he ate locusts and wild honey." So? This is the exact same clothing worn by Elijah in 2 Kings 1:8. John knew who he was. He knew his purpose. Not only did he avoid certain things, but John also did certain things that fit with his calling. Do even the smallest details of your life—what you eat and wear—line up with God's will?

Finally, read Luke 3:7-20. Today, it's easy to fall into the same deadly pit as the "brood of vipers"

John challenged here. Many people claim to be a Christian; they go to church and have even been baptized, but nothing has changed. John said: PROVE IT; LIVE IT. Simply put, a person's life should have clear evidence of being different. To repent means to turn the opposite direction; so are you living counter-culturally?

Write down the sacrifices made/prices paid by John.

What specific instructions did John provide in Luke 3?

all for the kingdom

What do these instructions have to do with you today? Write, in your own words, what God is calling you to do.

The truth John spoke and the lifestyle he led resulted in some people mocking and hating him, and ultimately his imprisonment. But John knew God's mission was worth it. Many other people listened to the truth he shared. Not only what you say you believe, but what you choose to do and don't do should line up with His call. God is calling you to be part of His mission in advancing the gospel of His Kingdom.

HAVE YOU EVER SEEN THOSE STRONG MEN COMPETITIONS? SOME GUY PULLS A CAR OR SOMETHING RIDICULOUS SUCH AS THAT. YES, IT OBVIOUSLY TAKES STRENGTH, BUT THE KEY IS PERSEVERANCE. THOSE GUYS DON'T JUST TAKE A RUNNING START AND RUN SMACK INTO IT OR LET IT YANK THEM DOWN...

but that's so often how we treat the mission of God. . . .

We get excited and in one excited burst of energy we throw ourselves at the world. When nothing seems to happen and nobody seems moved we sit stunned, shaking our head. It hurts. We can't believe it didn't work.

Instead, we have to lean into the will of God and steadily pull against a stubborn world. It starts to get easier once things get rolling, but it will never be easy. It will always require strength that only He can provide. Don't get discouraged. And don't take a break either.

IT'S NOT IMPOSSIBLE.

don't give up.

devotion.

The checkout line is littered with them . . . gossip magazines and bizarre tabloids. Cheap photo tricks, made up news, shocking headlines, and heartless jabs. These magazines aren't concerned with journalistic integrity to say the least; they're out for blood and money. It doesn't matter who gets hurt in the process, as long as you buy into the hype. The paparazzi are like snipers, poaching celebrity privacy in the hunt for some juicy scandal or dirty little secret. If they can't dig one up, they'll create one. Relationships, body image, steroids—whatever. The worse, the better. If a public figure is going to survive today's media-saturated climate, he or she needs to learn how to tune out the noise. (It also helps to actually stay out of trouble!)

First read Nehemiah 4:1–3. God's people endured some real critics. The harshness of the ridicule may get lost in translation, but the Jews were seriously harassed. Sanballat led the charge, rallying support from the wealthy and influential establishment. But Nehemiah was not discouraged. Now read Nehemiah 6:5–9. When mockery didn't prove to be a sufficient deterrent, Sanballat began writing lies. Again, Nehemiah ignored the lies, dismissing the false accusations as existing only in his enemies' mind. Instead of giving up, Nehemiah rose to meet the challenge, praying for God's strength. The result: He saw the impossible made possible.

Whether you like it or not, whether you think it's fair or unfair, people are watching you. If you start taking this "God thing" seriously, people aren't going to be cool with it. But when insults and rumors begin spreading about your radical lifestyle and impossibly idealistic perspective, what will you do? Will you cave, crumbling under the pressure like the rubble of an old wall, or will you pray for God's strength to complete the mission He has given you?

WHAT MIGHT people say to DISCOURAGE you from pursuing this DREAM? Write down any criticism, "advice," doubts, or ridicule that someone may say to NEGATIVELY INFLUENCE you.

You have dreams. Hopes. Passions. Burdens. Righteous anger. These are God-given gifts that are all part of your calling. This is who God made you for His purpose. So what is it that excites you or infuriates you spiritually? What brings tears of joy or sympathy to your eyes? What is it inside of you that fills you with hope or kills you when you think about it? Use this space to begin identifying God's call on your life. Write down the things that may seem impossible, that you would most love to see happen? What needs to change? What needs to happen? What would you need to do? What would God need to do?

reverb
reverb
reverb
261

*Turn the page to keep record of God's promises. . . . His voice is the one you must listen to.

open letter

Nehemiah's critics sent an open letter, inventing lies about him. They wanted to discredit the work God had given him to complete. Later, in the New Testament, Paul says that our lives as believers are open letters, testifying to the truth. Nobody can discredit the work of the gospel in your life and the mission of God's Spirit.

"You yourselves are our letter, written on our hearts, known and read by everybody. You show that you are a letter from Christ, the result of our ministry, written not with ink but with the Spirit of the living God, not on tablets of stone but on tablets of human hearts. Such confidence as this is ours through Christ before God. Not that we are competent in ourselves to claim anything for ourselves, but our competence comes from God."
(2 Corinthians 3:2-5)

Write down any Scriptures you can find that encourage you to pursue God's will for your life, no matter how impossible it may seem or what other people say. Try looking up key words in your concordance and using cross-references on any verses you find. See where that trail leads you. Listed below are a few verses to get you started.

Luke 1:37-38

Isa. 41:10

Jer. 33:3

Jer. 29:11

Eph. 2:10

Hab. 1:5

Phil. 4:13

Rom. 11:29

Nehemiah faced a serious challenge. He was heavily burdened by the condition of God's people. Sinfulness (disregard for God's Word) had led them to a state of exile; they were under the rule of foreign authority and the walls of Jerusalem lay in ruin. With great conviction, Nehemiah devoted himself to God's mission instead of his personal ambition. It would have been easy for him to accept his position in life as royal cupbearer, serving the king, but Nehemiah knew that nothing was more important than serving the King of kings and making His name known. God's people needed a reminder of God's call to be set apart from the culture surrounding them.

So he did two key things worth paying attention to today. Read Nehemiah 2:4-6.

He prayed and he planned. Before meeting with the king, Nehemiah poured his heart out to God, confessing any sin and asking for God's power and strength to complete the task ahead. While talking to the king, Nehemiah was praying in the middle of their conversation. When the king asked for details of the plan, Nehemiah was prepared with a definite time. He was both spiritual and practical; he was following God's lead while also taking initiative.

What would happen if you were "too spiritual" and never did anything but pray?

What would happen if you were "too practical" and never prayed about anything?

sacrifice.

Now read Nehemiah 4:7-9. When God's mission took Nehemiah into the midst of a hostile environment, he again responded with prayer and a plan. Trusting God and depending on Him does not mean that we are not responsible for taking action. When God calls us to do His work, He calls us to not only use our hearts, but our minds and our strength as well. Read about the balance of faith and action in verses 16-23. They trusted God to fight for them, but they always carried their weapons, too. They depended on God's strength to rebuild the wall, but they continually worked on it.

Read about the result in Nehemiah 6:9, 15-16.

Do you find yourself being "too spiritual," yet never taking any action or initiative on what you say you believe? Or do you tend to make your own plans without consulting God's will for the direction you should take? Pray now, and write down some practical steps for making sure you live fully devoted to serving God's Kingdom and enduring resistance from the world. (The world will not like it when you start to put your faith into action to see change.) How will you remember to pray? How will you take action? How will you not get discouraged when people make fun of you or harass you?

there are windows of
opportunity everywhere.

reverb
reverb
reverb
265

devotion.

"Be Prepared." This has been the Scout motto for 100 years. Millions of young people around the world have been raised to be ready for any opportunity that may present itself . . . at least in theory. (Tying and untying knots may not be quite as essential a skill as it was back in the day.) From Hank Aaron to Steven Spielberg, Martha Stewart to Bill Gates, people from all kinds of backgrounds grew up with this simple idea echoing in their minds. But maybe Scouts was never your thing. Sure, the cookies may be great but badges and uniforms had zero appeal. Regardless of how comfortable you feel in shorts and tall socks, the concept of being prepared is one we all need to embrace.

Read Acts 8:26-40. Philip was prepared to obey God immediately, going to a desert road and then running up to a man traveling home. When Philip approached the Ethiopian eunuch, he stepped right into a situation to share the story of Jesus. He was prepared to answer the man's question about Scripture. When the royal official responded to the gospel in faith, Philip was prepared to baptize the new believer.

Then, he was on his way again, ready to go anywhere God led Him and to talk with anyone who crossed his path.

Are you prepared? If God provided the opportunities would you be able to step in and respond with faith and obedience? With Philip, God provided the direction, the opportunity, and the perfect timing. (They just happened to be passing water in the desert deep enough for both of them to go down into for baptism!) Are you listening to the Spirit, looking for God to open doors, and running through them when He does? When opportunity knocks, are you prepared to share the good news of Jesus Christ anytime, anywhere, with anyone?

"WAKE UP, O SLEEPER, RISE FROM THE DEAD, AND CHRIST WILL SHINE ON YOU." Be very careful, then, how you live—not as unwise but as wise, making the most of every opportunity, because the days are evil. Therefore do not be foolish, but understand what the Lord's will is."
—EPHESIANS 5:14-17

ARE YOU MAKING THE MOST OF EVERY OPPORTUNITY?

DO YOU UNDERSTAND WHAT THE LORD'S WILL IS?

OR ARE YOU SLEEPING through your days?

PRAY FOR WISDOM. PRAY FOR OPEN EYES. PRAY FOR ACTION.

Jewish laws would have forbidden the foreign eunuch from entering the Temple to worship. He was outside of the religious circle. God sent Philip to meet him in the desert. Sometimes churches and youth groups can become the religious circles of today. People get left out. Maybe you've seen this. Maybe you've experienced this. Maybe you're on the outside looking in. If so, know that God will send someone to you. Don't let the circle discourage you. Or maybe you're on the inside looking out. Get out of your bubble. Reach out to anyone who is left out. You may be surprised at what God does in both your life and theirs once you do reach out to them.

The Book of Acts contains story after story about the early Church. Throughout the book are situations that seem chaotic or threatening, but prove to be no obstacle for God's mission. The gospel of Jesus Christ advances no matter what the world throws in its way. In Acts 6, the church in Jerusalem (kind of the Christian head-quarters at that time) chose additional leaders to help the apostles since so many people were coming to faith. Two of the helpers chosen were Stephen and Philip. Chapter 7 is all about Steven, who liter-ally gave his life to see God's will accomplished. Chapter 8 focuses on Philip.

Read Acts 8:4-5. Now jump over to read verse 25. Now jump over to read verse 40. Write down all the similarities in these Scriptures. How would you sum these up in your own words?

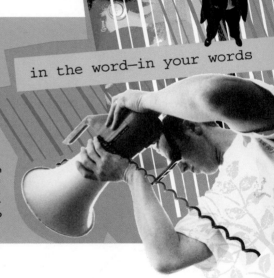

in the word—in your words

The people scattering from Jerusalem was the result of intense persecution lead by Saul, who would later surrender his life to Jesus and then be known as Paul (Read chapter 9 later). Most of the remain-der of Acts is about Paul's missionary jour-neys. Similar to Philip, Paul would share the gospel with anyone he met, wherever God had him at the time. In chapter 16, Paul recruited a helper named Timothy.

Read Paul's encouragement to the young disciple in 2 Timothy 3:10-4:2. In every situation they experi-enced, the Lord brought them through it. Paul made it very clear that there would be difficult times for anyone who surrenders to God's call and follows Christ. Paul gave specific instructions to Timothy in 3:14-4:2. In your own words, how would you sum up the importance of knowing the Bible?

If our lives are going to make an eternal impact, if we are going to live for Christ, then we must keep learning more and more about His Word. Scripture contains the life-changing message of the gospel—the truth that saves people, the breath of God that equips us for every good work. Always be ready, every day of the year. Now, read one last Scripture, 1 Peter 3:15. Rewrite this verse as your prayer to conclude this activity. Are you ready for any question a friend, teacher, family member, or stranger may ask? Could someone ask: "What is differ-ent about you? How and why do you live the way you do?" Write your prayer now, using the words of Peter and Paul and the example of Philip; pray that you would be ready to share the gospel in word and in deed at all times.

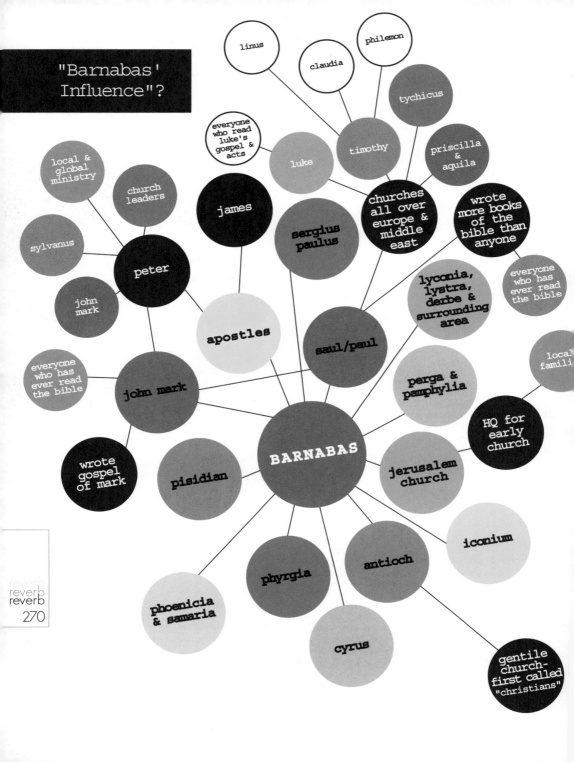

"Barnabas' Influence"?

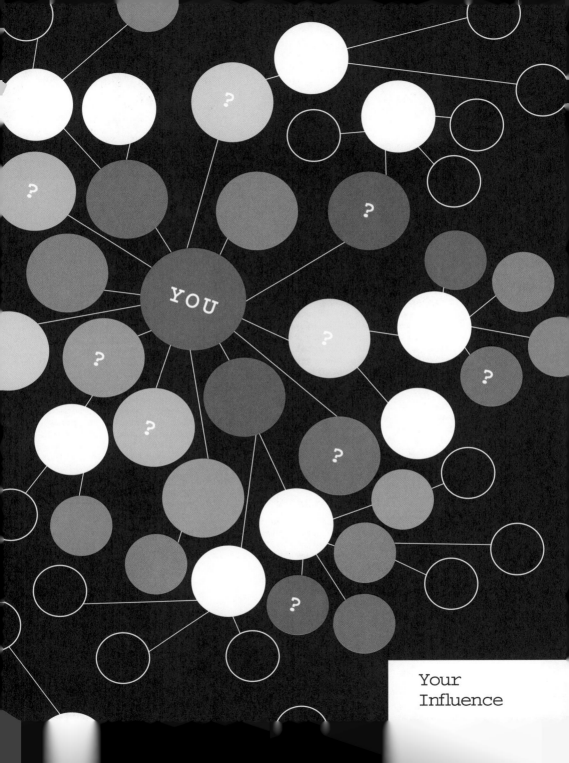

YOU

Your
Influence

devotion.

What do Heath Ledger as the Joker in *The Dark Knight* (2008) and Jennifer Hudson as Effie in *Dreamgirls* (2006) have in common? Nothing at first glance, they couldn't be more opposite. But as unique as these characters seem in their movies, each won the Academy Award™ for best supporting role. Neither of the stories would be the same without their contributions. In fact, though neither of these actors played their respective plots' main character, this is quite possibly the person who comes to mind as making the film truly great.

Similarly, it would be hard to argue against a guy named Barnabas being the obvious frontrunner if such an award existed in the New Testament. Although, if he were given a little gold statue, he would probably sell it and give the money away! (Read Acts 4:36–37 to see why.)

Every time Barnabas is mentioned in Scripture, he is encouraging someone else, supporting God's bigger story, and enabling others to play their parts. He is not fighting for the spotlight; he is simply fulfilling his role in the mission. Now turn over and read Acts 11:19–30.

Barnabas had a reputation for being trustworthy, generous, and supportive. He did whatever was needed at the time and many lives were changed as a result.

What about your role in God's mission? How are you known? If you are a Christ-follower, then you are part of His story now. Are you willing to play whatever part is necessary, following the Spirit's direction? There are people in your life that need to be encouraged. They need to not only hear about God's grace, but to also experience it through your generosity. Your life is not about you. Jesus is the Hero. You play a supporting role in the greatest adventure of love and mystery ever known. Give everything you've got to make the story of Christ famous TODAY.

who has your back?

who is surrounding you?

WHO IS SUPPORTING YOU?

WHO ARE YOU LIFTING UP?

who is your strength when you are tired?

who helps carry your burdens?

WHO DO YOU LOOK UP TO?

WHO LOOKS UP TO YOU?

your life isn't a solo

no matter what you think, you
need others and they need you.
It's part of God's plan...

HE DESIGNED IT THIS WAY.

Barnabas spent his life loving God by loving people, using both his personality and his possessions for God's purpose. We are first introduced to Barnabas in Acts 4:32-37. You're familiar with it, but read it again now. The first Church in Jerusalem experienced incredible community; they took care of each other's needs—both spiritual and physical. If everyone was living with this selfless mindset, yet Barnabas was mentioned by name, his grace and generosity must have been truly exceptional.

He sold property (most likely in Cyprus, since he was a Levite and by law could not own land in Jerusalem) and gave every penny to the church in Jerusalem to use as needed. This generosity and encouragement was in stark contrast to a couple who later gave money to the church (Ananias and Sapphira in Acts 5:1-11). They lied; however, their sin was not in keeping some of the money, but in faking generosity. They were giving to be seen by people as opposed to Barnabas who gave to help people see God. God doesn't need our money, but He knows how to use it better than we do on our own. Surrendering yourself completely to His mission means you give all of your personality and possessions for His purpose, encouraging others to grow in their faith.

Read the following passages of Scripture and answer the question for each.

POSSESSIONS
(Matthew 6:19-24) Jesus didn't say that it is wrong to have possessions or that a certain economic status is more holy than another. What He said was that you can't "serve" both masters or store up your treasure in both eternal and temporary things. How are you seeking opportunities to encourage others with your possessions?

PERSONALITY
(Colossians 3:12-17, 23) Everyone is supposed to have the character of Christ's Spirit, described in verses 12-16. We should all look the same in these areas. But verses 17 and 23 emphasize that we're all unique, and so "whatever you do" should be done for Christ. How well do the specifics of this list describe you? Write down some unique things you are good at and like to do. Now, how will you do those things in a way that encourages you and others to grow in Christ?

PURPOSE
(Ephesians 4:1-13) Using our different gifts, abilities, and resources, we all have the same purpose and calling. We're to encourage and equip each other on God's mission.

posessions, personality, purpose

"My purpose in life is to"
(summarize verses 12-13)

"I will do this by"
(summarize verses 2-3)

Let's face it: There are times in life when the going gets pretty tough. This is true for anyone. It's true regardless of your ethnicity, your geography, or your religious preference. But it is all the more true for Christ-followers living their lives on mission for God. You can relate to this, right?

Have you walked through life's valleys? Has the world beat you up for your convictions? Do you ever feel like everyone is against you? Well, don't get down. You see, you serve a Lord who experienced all the same things . . . and much, much more. Because the world hated Him, it will hate you as well. But the cool thing is that He won victory over the world, which means you have, too. However, you still have to fight the fight . . . which is what *Squeeze* is all about. If you're ready to get in the ring, turn the page.

- **Session 1:** The Real ENEMY —Pg 278-283
- **Session 2:** The ENEMY Within —Pg 284-289
- **Session 3:** Going on the DEFENSE —Pg 290-295
- **Session 4:** Loving the UNLOVABLE —Pg 296-301
- **Session 5:** PUSH Through It —Pg 302-307
- **Session 6:** MORE Than On Our Own —Pg 308-313

You naturally avoid conflict. Everything about you says to flee danger. To seek safety. To place yourself in situations where you have control. People who seek out potentially harmful situations go against the grain of society.

Yet, by committing to following Christ you are guaranteeing yourself conflict. You are pitting yourself head-on against the ways of the world.

CONFLICT WITH THE WORLD? BRING IT ON.

DEVOTION

History is full of examples of undeserved persecution.

During the Russian Civil War nearly 500,000 Cossacks were killed or deported by the Bolsheviks.

At one time in the history of both South Africa and the United States, having black skin meant an individual was a second-class citizen.

In World War II, the Nazis sought to exterminate the Jews simply due to their ethnic origin.

The U.S. Government decimated the Native American population in the 19th century in an effort to take over their land.

In each of these cases, and in the numerous other instances of persecution, the parties being persecuted did nothing to deserve the treatment they experienced. The persecution was unjust, unexpected, and completely unfounded.

There is a different kind of persecution going on all over the world today. This persecution is ages old. And it was predicted thousands of years ago. Yet, it goes on today . . . still. The interesting thing is that you might have even experienced it.

What is this persecution? It is the persecution Christ-followers experience because of the name of Jesus. Maybe you've had conflict in your life because you identify yourself as a follower of Jesus. If you have ever stood up for your faith, and someone made fun of or marginalized you because of it, then you know what it means to feel rejected because of Christ.

But this should come as no surprise to you. In fact, Jesus predicted it long ago. Read John 15:18–25 and John 16:33. People hated Jesus simply because He was God's Son. Jesus knew this. And He knew that people would hate you because you follow God's Son. While it might not seem fair or logical, it is part of the truth of being a disciple of Jesus.

So how should you respond? Pray for those who persecute you. Live a life of obedience and commitment to God regardless of what happens. And take confidence in Jesus' words recorded in John chapter 16:

"In this world you will have trouble. But take heart!
I have overcome the world."

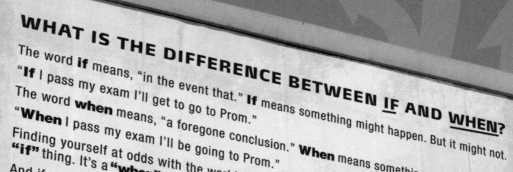

WHAT IS THE DIFFERENCE BETWEEN <u>IF</u> AND <u>WHEN</u>?

The word **if** means, "in the event that." **If** means something might happen. But it might not.

"**If** I pass my exam I'll get to go to Prom."

The word **when** means, "a foregone conclusion." **When** means something is a sure thing.

"**When** I pass my exam I'll be going to Prom."

Finding yourself at odds with the world around you simply because you follow Jesus is not an "**if**" thing. It's a **"when"** thing.

And if you have never been in a position where the world has turned against you because of your faith, you might need to ask yourself this question:

"Am I truly living the life of a Christ-follower?"

Editor's Note: By way of an amazing top-secret government technology, we were able to conduct interviews with Christians who have been murdered due to their faith. The following transcript was taken from our reporter's interview with Ignatius, Bishop of Antioch.

Reporter: So, via this amazing technology, I am actually talking with Ignatius, Bishop of Antioch. Bishop, is this sort of odd for you?

Ignatius: Yeah, I mean, this is all kind of crazy, you know? After all, I have been dead for 1900 years. But it's great to be talking with you.

Reporter: So, give me the quick update on your background. Tell me about your early life.

Ignatius: Well, I was hanging out in Antioch worshipping at the Church there. You might not know this, but I knew John the Apostle *and* Peter.

Reporter: Really?

Ignatius: You betcha.

Reporter: Those guys must have been pretty cool.

Ignatius: Well, actually, we were all pretty warm most of the time. Antioch is kind of a temperate climate, you know. Dusty, too. The dry air is murder on your hair.

Reporter: Yeah . . . sure. Um, so, tell me about the occasion surrounding your martyrdom. If that's OK.

Ignatius: Oh, it's fine. I never get tired of telling the story. Quite simply, I was arrested because of my belief in Jesus Christ. I was taken to Rome from my home in Syria. Oh, that was an awful trip! I was bound in chains and was alongside exotic animals that were being taken to Rome, as well. I was fighting for my life the whole trip!

Reporter: That must have been horrible. Did you ever think about denying your faith? Or just giving up?

Ignatius: Never! Why would I ever dream of such a thing? Christ gave Himself for all sinners in an equally torturous manner. I was committed to standing strong.

Reporter: You were actually fed to the lions in the Coliseum in Rome by the emperor Trajan. I don't know if you know this, but he said later that he thought he would make an example of you. He thought that other Christians would deny Christ when they saw you murdered.

Ignatius: *[Ignatius lets out a long sigh]* I expected as much. Tell me, did it work? Did others deny their faith?

Reporter: Well, I can't say that *no one* denied their faith in Christ, but I can tell you that hundreds of millions of people have lost their lives for the sake of Christ since the day you died in AD 108. All of these people would rather die than deny Christ.

Ignatius: You know . . . I *knew* it wouldn't work. I *knew* Christians would stay strong. You can't imagine how happy that makes me.

Reporter: Glad I could brighten your day. Ignatius, thanks for talking with us.

Ignatius: Sure. No problem.

"I am writing to all the Churches and I enjoin all, that I am dying willingly for God's sake, if only you do not prevent it. I beg you, do not do me an untimely kindness. Allow me to be eaten by the beasts, which are my way of reaching to God. I am God's wheat, and I am to be ground by the teeth of wild beasts, so that I may become the pure bread of Christ."
— Ignatius, Letter to the Romans

What does PERSECUTION look like?

This chapter of the book obviously focuses on persecution and the difficulties you face in this life due to your faith in Christ. This activity is designed to help you start thinking about persecution in the world around you.

Let's start by writing a definition. In your own words, what is persecution?

Persecution looks different for everyone. If you are a Christian in Eritrea right now, persecution for you might mean a prison sentence accompanied by torture. If you live in Boston, Massachusetts, persecution for you might mean getting made fun of or not getting invited to parties.

What does persecution look like for you in your world? Describe times when you or someone you know has experienced persecution due to faith in Jesus.

Is there a right way or a wrong way to react to persecution? Think about it, and then explain your answer.

Read in Philippians 1:12–14 what Paul wrote from prison. How do Paul's words address the idea that persecution can actually have positive results?

Here's the deal with persecution: God does not call us to go looking for it. But we should know that if we are living the life we are called to live, we will experience it. Thankfully, God will never leave us alone to experience it. The Holy Spirit is always with us, especially in the midst of trials.

Be bold in your faith and expect to find yourself in conflict with the world.

YOU THINK YOU'RE THE ONLY ONE WHO HAS EVER HAD PEOPLE TALK ABOUT YOU BECAUSE OF YOUR FAITH? WELL, THINK AGAIN. JESUS HAD PLENTY OF PEOPLE AGAINST HIM. HERE ARE JUST A FEW EXAMPLES:

Then the Pharisees went out and began to plot with the Herodians how they might kill Jesus. — **Mark 3:6**

And when the demon was driven out, the man who had been mute spoke. The crowd was amazed and said, "Nothing like this has ever been seen in Israel." But the Pharisees said, "It is by the prince of demons that he drives out demons." — **Matthew 9:33-34**

The Pharisees and the teachers of the law were looking for a reason to accuse Jesus, so they watched him closely to see if he would heal on the Sabbath. — **Luke 6:7**

Then the Pharisees went out and laid plans to trap him in his words. — **Matthew 22:15**

Then some Pharisees and teachers of the law came to Jesus from Jerusalem and asked, "Why do your disciples break the tradition of the elders? They don't wash their hands before they eat!" — **Matthew 15:1-2**

Later they sent some of the Pharisees and Herodians to Jesus to catch him in his words. — **Mark 12:13**

When the teachers of the law who were Pharisees saw him eating with the "sinners" and tax collectors, they asked his disciples: "Why does he eat with tax collectors and 'sinners'?" — **Mark 2:16**

Some Pharisees came to him to test him. They asked, "Is it lawful for a man to divorce his wife for any and every reason?" — **Matthew 19:3**

When Jesus left there, the Pharisees and the teachers of the law began to oppose him fiercely and to besiege him with questions, waiting to catch him in something he might say. — **Luke 11:53-54**

Then some of the Pharisees and teachers of the law said to him, "Teacher, we want to see a miraculous sign from you." He answered, "A wicked and adulterous generation asks for a miraculous sign!" — **Matthew 12:38-39**

When the chief priests and the Pharisees heard Jesus' parables, they knew he was talking about them. They looked for a way to arrest him, but they were afraid of the crowd because the people held that he was a prophet. — **Matthew 21:45-46**

The Pharisees and the teachers of the law began thinking to themselves, "Who is this fellow who speaks blasphemy? Who can forgive sins but God alone?" — **Luke 5:21**

Do you ever feel like you are your own worst enemy? Do you ever want to just cry out to God, "Save me from myself!" If you feel this way, you are not alone. This battle has been waged in the hearts and minds of Christ-followers throughout the history of humankind. The heroes of the Old Testament struggled with it. The heroes of the New Testament struggled with it.

In fact, there was only One who hasn't. And the cool thing about it? By defeating death and sin, He has given you the power to overcome the battle that wages within you.

DEVOTION

Do you know people who look as if they have it all together? You can see how close they are to God and how awesome their lives seem. You say to yourself, "I wish I were just like them." Here's a little secret: Even the most spiritually mature Christ-followers sin . . . all the time. And while you should have people in your life who are spiritual mentors, it's important to realize that no one is good enough in him or herself to live a sin-free life.

Why? Because all people have what's called a "sin nature." This is the part of us that seeks to look out for ourselves first. This is the part of ourselves that we do battle with. Our sin nature is where temptation becomes reality. No one is immune to it. Not even the strongest Christ-followers you know. Not even the Apostle Paul.

Paul wrote an awesome passage about this in his letter to the Romans. You can read the entire passage in Romans 7:14–8:2. But here's a paraphrase of a part of it from The Message paraphrase. In this section, Paul was talking about the internal battle with his sin nature. See if you can relate to his struggle:

"For if I know the law but still can't keep it, and if the power of sin within me keeps sabotaging my best intentions, I obviously need help! I realize that I don't have what it takes. I can will it, but I can't do it. I decide to do good, but I don't really do it; I decide not to do bad, but then I do it anyway. My decisions, such as they are, don't result in actions. Something has gone wrong deep within me and gets the better of me every time. It happens so regularly that it's predictable. The moment I decide to do good, sin is there to trip me up. I truly delight in God's commands, but it's pretty obvious that not all of me joins in that delight. Parts of me covertly rebel, and just when I least expect it, they take charge." —Romans 7:17–23

Can you relate to Paul? Have you ever felt like there were times when no matter how hard you try, you just could not control your sin nature? What can you do in these times to keep from falling over and over again? Thankfully, Paul gives us some advice:

"I've tried everything and nothing helps. I'm at the end of my rope. Is there no one who can do anything for me? Isn't that the real question? The answer, thank God, is that Jesus Christ can and does. He acted to set things right in this life of contradictions where I want to serve God with all my heart and mind, but am pulled by the influence of sin to do something totally different." —Romans 7:24–25

Jesus has set you free from the power of sin. While you will always battle with your sin nature, take comfort in the fact that Christ has ultimately defeated the power of sin over the world. He has given you the strength to fight when you think you cannot fight anymore. Next time you find yourself in the struggle, stop and thank Jesus for providing you with a way out.

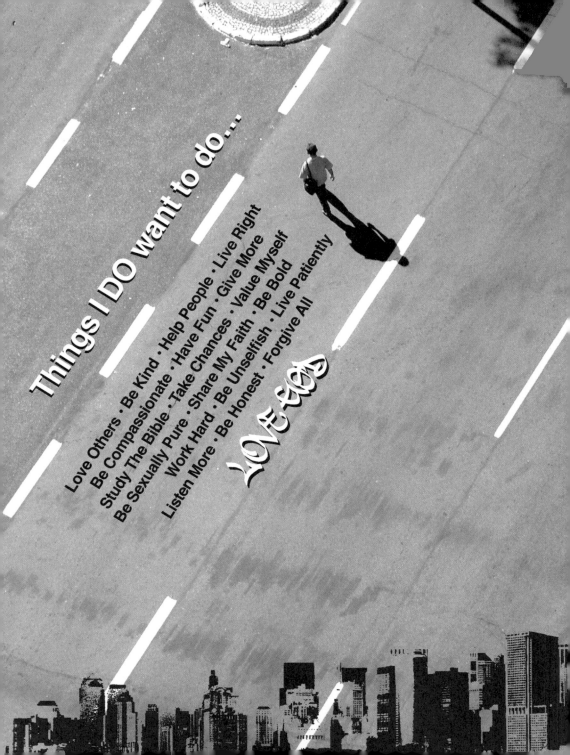

Things I DO want to do...

Love Others • Be Kind • Help People • Live Right
Be Compassionate • Have Fun • Give More
Study The Bible • Take Chances • Value Myself
Be Sexually Pure • Share My Faith • Be Bold
Work Hard • Be Unselfish • Live Patiently
Listen More • Be Honest • Forgive All

LOVE GOD

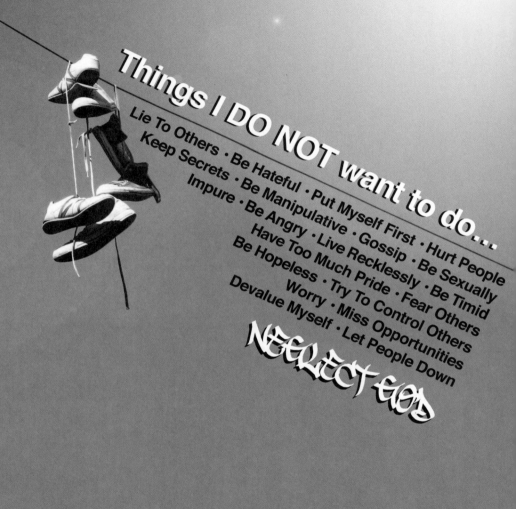

Things I DO NOT want to do...

Lie To Others · Be Hateful · Put Myself First · Hurt People
Keep Secrets · Be Manipulative · Gossip · Be Sexually
Impure · Be Angry · Live Recklessly · Be Timid
Have Too Much Pride · Fear Others
Be Hopeless · Try To Control Others
Worry · Miss Opportunities
Devalue Myself · Let People Down

NEGLECT GOD

So, you want to do the right things but you're struggling with consistency. Well, don't beat yourself up too much. It's pretty common. But you must attempt to deal with whatever's tripping you up. Use the chart below and see if it helps you.

Column 1	Column 2	Column 3	Column 4
Things I Do (But Don't Want To)	Reasons It's Hard To Stop	Ways I Can Address Column 2	Successes and Failure

INSTRUCTIONS

- In Column 1, write something you struggle with. If you don't want to write it out, use an abbreviation that only you would understand.
- In Column 2, write some of the reasons why it's hard for you to stop doing whatever it is you don't want to do.
    - o Pray that God would help reveal to you reasons why it's hard for you to quit.
- In Column 3, come up with some ways to address Column 2. Try and figure out ways you can alleviate some of the reasons why it is hard to quit.
    - o Pray for the Spirit's help in dealing with this issue.
- Column 4 is for you to track your progress. If you had a bad day, write it down. If you had a good day, write it down.

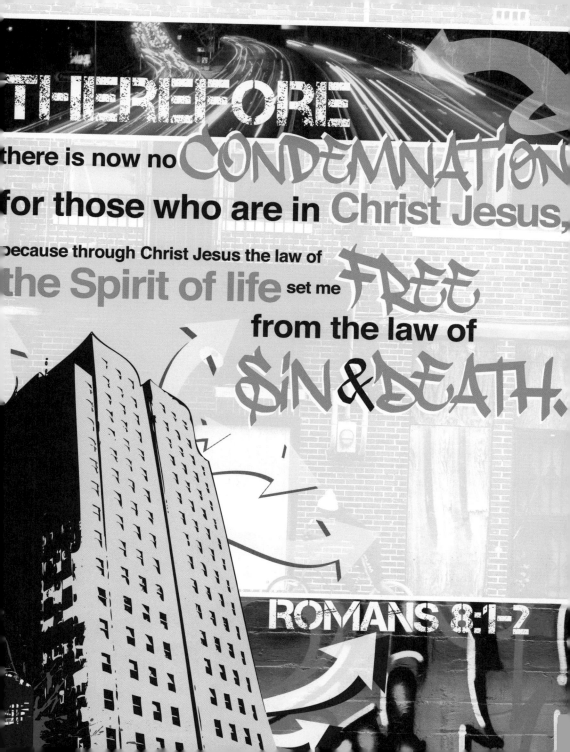

THEREFORE there is now no CONDEMNATION for those who are in Christ Jesus, because through Christ Jesus the law of the Spirit of life set me FREE from the law of SIN & DEATH.

ROMANS 8:1-2

Do Not Enter! Wrong Way! Keep Out! Warning!

The signs we see in the world around us give notice to the danger ahead. If we're smart, we'll follow these signs. In many cases, they are there to protect us from something we are not prepared to handle.

Your life as a Christ-follower is similar in one way: There is danger ahead. You will be pitted against evil and against a hostile culture. If your faith worked like the world, there would be a sign that read, "Danger Ahead! Keep Out!" But your faith doesn't work like that. God has equipped you to fight anything that comes your way.

Yes, there is danger ahead. But you've got the King of Kings on your side.

Danger, here I come . . .

SPORT

Defense Wins It Again!

TITLETOWN, USA—If you follow sports you might have heard the saying, "Offense wins games; defense wins championships." This is true in many different sports. In order to be successful you must have a good offense. But a good offense without a good defense usually isn't enough to win the ultimate prize.

In sports, a good defense is vital. This is true in our spiritual lives as well.

Let's face it, you're in a battle. You're at war with the dark forces of this world. Satan wants to keep as much distance between you and God as possible. He will do this by coming at you with every temptation imaginable.

But God has equipped you to resist Satan's attacks. He has not left you defenseless.

In sports, a good defense can stop the most powerful offenses.

In your spiritual life, no matter how hard Satan tries, God has given you the means to defend yourself.

The plan is laid out for you in God's Word. However, it's up to you to execute it.

THIS IS NOT YOU.

THOUGH

YOU WILL FACE PRESSURE,

YOU WILL NOT BE

CRUSHED.

GOD WON'T LET THAT HAPPEN.

THE ARMOR OF GOD

The Apostle Paul understood conflict with the world. Paul had been stoned and left for dead, whipped, beaten, and run out of various cities, all because he willingly gave his life to serve Christ.

One of the most well-known passages of the New Testament is Paul's description of the spiritual armor of God. In describing it, Paul helps us see that not only is our battle a real one against evil, but that God has equipped us to be victorious. Let's take a closer look.

Open your Bible to Ephesians 6:10–18, and keep it open to work your way through the following activity. **Read Ephesians 6:10–12.** Paul did a cool job of providing perspective on the nature of conflict. What did Paul say in verse 12 that speaks to who the real enemy is?

Paul said the real enemy is not other people ("flesh and blood"), but the evil spiritual forces at work in this world. How might this shift in perspective help you deal with people who seem to be your enemies?

In verse 11, the Greek word Paul used for "full armor," is the term used for the full equipment, both defensive and offensive, of the heavily armed Roman foot soldier. Some scholars have even guessed that Paul was writing this letter while looking at a Roman soldier. (Remember, Paul was in jail at the time.) So, when Paul talked about going into battle, he wasn't joking.

Read Ephesians 6:14. Roman soldiers would fasten their clothing securely around their waist with a belt. This made quick movements easier and was crucial to their ability to fight in combat. How does knowing the truth of God's Word help your ability to respond quickly to trials?

The Roman soldier's breastplate was a metal piece that protected the chest, lungs, and heart. How does living a good (righteous) life protect you from those who want to bring you down?

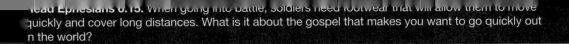

Read Ephesians 6:15. When going into battle, soldiers need footwear that will allow them to move quickly and cover long distances. What is it about the gospel that makes you want to go quickly out in the world?

Read Ephesians 6:16. Roman soldiers had a large, oblong shield made of two large pieces of wood. This shield was used for defensive purposes, oftentimes for defense from the enemy's flaming arrows. In what ways does your faith help defend you from Satan's arrows of temptation?

Read Ephesians 6:17. The Roman soldier's helmet served the same purpose helmets serve today: it protected the soldier's head. How does your salvation in Christ protect you from the doubts, fears, and impure thoughts that sometimes enter your mind?

The Greek word Paul used for sword was the short, sharp sword crucial for Roman soldiers fighting in close combat. The sword is the only offensive weapon Paul mentioned. How can you depend on God's Word to help you make it through tough situations?

How cool is it that you have all the available tools to help you withstand the persecution of the world? God has given you the ability to stay strong. He wants you to stay in the fight. Next time the world seems like it is against you, remember these verses and stand tall. With God by your side, you can do it!

We all know them.

Some of them we must deal with daily. Others, we only observe from afar. Who is "them"? The people we dislike, that's who. People who get on our nerves. People who actively seek to make our lives miserable. People who seem to love being enemies of the world around them. People who seem easy to dislike.

Here's the problem: Jesus didn't give us the option of disliking anyone. Sure, you might never be BFF with the guy who started that awful rumor about you. But Jesus said that you couldn't keep any hateful feelings about him in your heart. This kind of teaching goes against everything the world teaches. But if you've learned anything so far, it's that being different from the world is a pretty good thing.

Let your enemies do what they will. YOU'RE READY

WHO IS MY ENEMY?

In Luke 6:27 Jesus said, "But I tell you who hear me: Love your enemies, do good to those who hate you."

Love your enemies. It's a bold commandment, isn't it? So bold, in fact, that we often ignore it. After all, how often do you show love to your enemies?

You might be saying to yourself, "I don't have any enemies. I'm crazy-nice to everyone I know." But if you stop thinking about enemies in terms of, say, Megatron, Darth Vader, or Osama bin Laden, you might find that you have some enemies in your life.

What is an enemy? A quick definition is "any individual who is opposed to you." The level of enemy might differ based on the level of opposition. But essentially, an enemy is anyone who is antagonistic toward you.

Now that you know the definition, how many of these folks do you have in your life? Better yet, how many of them do you love?

If you're like most people, you probably have some people in your life who seem to always be pitted against you. For whatever reason, they like to see you fail. And again, if you are like most people, you probably don't care for these folks. You might even think they're worthy of your dislike. They might act so nasty toward you that the only thing they seemingly deserve is your hatred.

Except that it doesn't work that way. It can't work that way.

You see, Romans 5:10 says, "For if, when we were God's enemies, we were reconciled to him through the death of his Son, how much more, having been reconciled, shall we be saved through his life!"

Did you catch that phrase? "When we were God's enemies." Yikes! That certainly doesn't feel good—to think about yourself as an enemy of God. But the truth is that before you accepted Christ's gift of grace and mercy, you were an enemy of God. Due to your sin nature, you were opposed to God. But He loved you so much, He sent His Son to provide a payment for your sinful ways.

If God loved you this much, there is absolutely no excuse for you to not go the extra distance to love others.

How can you begin to turn your anger and dislike toward those who oppose you into compassion and mercy? Pray that God would begin to soften your heart and convict you concerning your attitude toward your enemies.

The world is full of people who deny, dismiss, or otherwise hate God and His Son, Jesus.

Here's proof:

God is dead.
Let us not understand by this that he does not exist or even that he no longer exists.

He is dead.
—Jean-Paul Sartre, French Philosopher

I do not believe in God because I do not believe in

𝕸𝖔𝖙𝖍𝖊𝖗 𝕲𝖔𝖔𝖘𝖊.

—Clarence Darrow, Noted American Lawyer

I do not believe in the divinity of Christ.
— William Howard Taft, US President

I don't have the evidence to PROVE that GOD DOESN'T EXIST, but I so strongly suspect that he DOESN'T that I don't want to WASTE MY TIME.
—Isaac Asimov, American author

THERE'S PROBABLY NO GOD.
NOW STOP WORRYING ABOUT IT AND GET ON WITH YOUR LIFE.
—SIGN ON ENGLAND BUSES

It's no fun to hear people speak out against God.

Yet, what did Jesus say about how you should treat those who mistreat you and your God?

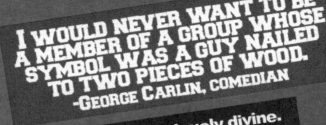

I WOULD NEVER WANT TO BE A MEMBER OF A GROUP WHOSE SYMBOL WAS A GUY NAILED TO TWO PIECES OF WOOD.
—GEORGE CARLIN, COMEDIAN

I cannot say that Jesus was uniquely divine. He was as much God as Krishna, or Rama, or Mohammed, or Zoroaster.
—Mahatma Gandhi, Indian religious leader

By the year 2000, we will, I hope, raise our children to believe in human potential, **not God.**

—Gloria Steinem, Women's Rights activist (1990)

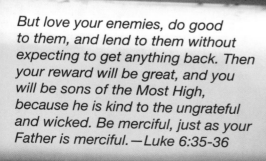

But love your enemies, do good to them, and lend to them without expecting to get anything back. Then your reward will be great, and you will be sons of the Most High, because he is kind to the ungrateful and wicked. Be merciful, just as your Father is merciful. —Luke 6:35-36

The Martyr Interviews, Part 2

Editors Note: By way of an amazing top-secret government technology, we were able to conduct interviews with Christians who have been murdered because of their faith. The following transcript is the second in the series of interviews, and was taken from an interview with our reporter and Dietrich Bonhoeffer, the great German theologian.

Reporter: OK, let's get started. For those of you who might have missed our earlier interview with Bishop Ignatius, these interviews are made possible by an amazing top-secret technology. Today I am speaking with Dietrich Bonhoeffer. Dr. Bonhoeffer, how are you?

Bonhoeffer: *Guten Morgen!* I am doing quite well, thank you for asking.

Reporter: Isn't this wild? I mean, you and me speaking to one another across time and space. After all, you died in 1945.

Bonhoeffer: No kidding . . . In all my years I couldn't have imagined it.

Reporter: Well, thank you so much for . . .

Bonhoeffer: *[interrupting]* Sorry for interrupting you, but before we move on, I have to ask: Was Hitler defeated? Please tell me the Germans were stopped.

Reporter: I should have told you, forgive me. I am happy to say that the Germans and the Japanese were defeated. The Nazi regime crumbled and was never heard from again. And the Japanese have become a significant and peaceful player in the global economy.

Bonhoeffer: Oh, praise God! Then it was all worth it.

Reporter: Well, Dr. Bonhoeffer, since you brought it up, let's talk about your story. You were a prominent theologian, teacher, and preacher in Germany in the years before World War II.

Bonhoeffer: That is correct.

Reporter: By 1941, the Nazi government had forbidden you to preach, teach, or even publish any writings. How did this make you feel?

Bonhoeffer: Well, I can tell you, I didn't like it one bit. And once I found out the monstrous things Hitler was doing to the Jews and others I knew he had to be stopped.

Reporter: You were part of the German resistance. You were arrested on April 6, 1943. During your time in prison you were a powerful minister to other prisoners and even to guards. But it was discovered that you knew about assassination attempts on Hitler. Even though you had nothing to do with the assassination, you were hanged on April 9, 1945.

Bonhoeffer: All of what you say is true. But you know, I have no regrets for the way I lived my life. Unto my death I maintained absolute love for God and confidence that His will would be done in the world.

Reporter: Well, I want you to know that the letters you wrote in prison were eventually published. Over the last 60 years your words have challenged Christ-followers all over the world and have shaped the way many people seek and understand God.

Bonhoeffer: That's great to know. All glory to God.

Reporter: Thank you, Dr. Bonhoeffer.

Bonhoeffer: *Mit tiefer Dankbarkeit!* The privilege was all mine.

"I saw Pastor Bonhoeffer . . . kneeling on the floor praying fervently to God. I was most deeply moved by the way this lovable man prayed, so devout and so certain that God heard his prayer. At the place of execution, he again said a short prayer and then climbed the few steps to the gallows, brave and composed. His death ensued after a few seconds. In the almost fifty years that I worked as a doctor, I have hardly ever seen a man die so entirely submissive to the will of God."
—Concentration Camp Doctor witnessing Bonhoeffer's death

HOW DOES LOVE LOOK?

Before the book is closed on the idea of loving those who persecute you, you have a little more work to do.

You've already thought about the concept of an enemy. (If you missed it, head back to page 297 and take a few minutes to catch up.) Now, you have to figure out exactly what it means to love them.

Keep in mind that this whole conversation started because of what Jesus said in Luke 6:27: "But I tell you who hear me: Love your enemies, do good to those who hate you." The important thing is to figure out just what Jesus wants us to do about dealing with those who definitely do not love us. After all, He said we were to love them, right?

You're probably aware that there are a few different Greek words for love in the New Testament. The word Jesus used here for love comes from the Greek word, agape (pronounced, uh-GAH-pay). The New Testament writers used agape to describe the perfect love of God for His Son (John 17:26). Agape was also used to describe the sacrificial love Jesus had for us, demonstrated by His death on the cross. Agape is the type of love that comes from God, a love that loves in spite of wrongdoings and a love that sacrifices everything for another person.

Sorry to break this to you, but this is the kind of love you are supposed to have for those who are against you. You are supposed to love your enemies sacrificially, in the perfect love of Christ. Ouch . . . This is not going to be easy, is it?

Honestly, this type of love for your enemies doesn't happen overnight. And it can't happen without prayer, commitment, and the power of the Holy Spirit. It might take a while, but if you stick with it, you can develop the kind of heart that seeks to show the love of Christ to those who are opposed to you.

Spend some time in prayer. Visualize the people who seem set against you. Now, say a prayer for those people. Pray that God will meet their needs. Finally, pray that your heart would be softened toward them. Pray that you would begin to love them in the spirit of God's love for you.

Trust the Lord to begin to change your heart. He will help you begin to show love to those who might seem unlovable. And through it all, you will bring honor and glory to God.

STAY STRONG

It's easy to get down. It's easy to look around you and want to give up. It's hard being a Christ-follower in a world set against you. No one is denying that. Some days it seems like it would be a lot easier—and maybe even more fun—to just throw away your beliefs, turn your back on your life, and follow the crowd.

DON'T BUY THE LIE

Life on this earth can be hard. (Ask Jesus. He knows a thing or two about that.) But victory comes in the fight. You don't have to defeat the world. He's already defeated it for you. You are called to fight. To stay in the race. To try when trying is the last thing you want to do. To persevere. To never quit. To never give up.

You are empowered with Spirit-given strength. Stay strong.

DEVOTION

Chances are you probably know that Mount Everest is the world's highest mountain. At 29,029 feet above sea level, Everest dominates the border of Nepal and Tibet. The first successful expedition to reach Everest's peak was led by New Zealand's Edmund Hillary and Nepal's Tenzing Norgay in May of 1953. It was an amazing feat of commitment and fortitude. In the years since the duo's famous ascent, over 4,000 other climbers have made it to the top of the majestic mountain. And while all of these climbers came from different countries, they all have one thing in common:

They didn't make it to the top of the mountain by focusing on what was *behind* them. They made it to the top by focusing on what was *ahead*.

Tackling Everest is such a difficult challenge that the only thing to keep climbers going is the promise of the summit. The prize of standing on the world's highest point keeps the climbers motivated. It helps them push through the most difficult terrain.

Stop for a moment and read Philippians 3:12–4:1. Philippians was one of Paul's "prison epistles," letters he wrote while under house arrest in Rome. When Paul wrote Philippians, he was nearing the end of his life and had experienced a tremendous amount of hardship and suffering, all for the sake of Jesus. But notice what he said here: Paul wasn't quitting. And he wasn't resting on his past accomplishments. What was he doing instead?

Verses 13–14 say it all: "Forgetting what is behind and straining toward what is ahead, I press on toward the goal to win the prize for which God has called me heavenward in Christ Jesus." Paul had not stopped pressing on toward the finish line. What was this finish line Paul talked about? Just like the summit of Everest motivates climbers to push on, the goal of living his entire life for Jesus motivated Paul to stay strong in his faith. He wasn't about to give up just because things got hard. He was concentrating on the goal.

You are called to live the exact same way. In a world that will happily knock you down because of your faith in Christ, you must be willing to pick yourself back up and press forward. God desires for you to live this way. And He has sent you His Spirit to keep you strong. There is nothing left for you to do but to face the goal and press onward. Keep climbing, keep running, and keep moving toward the goal of a powerful life lived for Christ.

In this particular section of the book, you have already looked at a passage from Paul's letter to the Philippians. This is one of those passages in Scripture so packed with awesome truth that you need to give it at least one more look before moving on. So, here's another chance to uncover a little more from Philippians 3.

In Philippians 3:17, Paul said something that is easy to skip over. But on closer examination, it is a profound piece of biblical application that, if followed, could dramatically affect your spiritual life.

Read verse 17 and rewrite the verse in your own words below:

Paul was asking his friends in Philippi to do two things: to look at his spiritual life as an example, and to look at the lives of other mature Christ-followers. This is a simple yet meaningful command. First of all, it says a lot about Paul's life, doesn't it?

By asking people to look to him as an example of how to live as a follower of Christ, what was Paul implying about his spiritual life?

Paul must have been so seriously devoted to Jesus that he had no problem telling people to imitate the way he followed Christ. Here's a question for you: **What would happen to someone if you told him or her to imitate your life as an example of what following Christ should look like? Don't just think about your answer, write it out:**

If you're like many people, you might not be fully comfortable asking someone to look to you as what it means to live the life of a Christ-follower. But here's the deal: It's never too late to change. God honors your commitment. Tell Him that you are going to be a more disciplined follower and follow through with it.

Finally, the other cool thing Paul said is that we should look to other more spiritually mature Christ-followers as examples. Here's the deal: God made us to be in community with one another. He never intended for you to try to live this life alone. **Think of the people in your life. List three or four or five individuals who are mature Christ-followers.**

Now, take the next step. Call one or two of these people and arrange a time to meet with them. Tell them that you desire to go deeper in your relationship with Christ. Ask them if they will agree to meet with you regularly and help you deal with the questions that will inevitably come up as you go through this life.

While Paul was not yet perfected, he was confident enough in his Christian walk to ask the Philippians to join in imitating him and other mature Christians. Much Christian growth comes through imitation of other Christians (Phil. 4:9; 1 Cor. 11:1; 2 Thess. 3:8–9; 1 Tim. 4:12, 15–16; 2 Tim. 3:10–11; Heb. 13:7; 1 Pet. 5:3).

PERSEVERANCE

Perseverance. It's a big word with a simple definition. It means, "to keep going in spite of opposition or discouragement." As a Christ-follower in this world, you will need perseverance. You will need it to keep going when the going gets tough.

Here are just a few verses that challenge you to hang in there when things get hard.

I give them eternal life, and they shall **never perish**; no one can snatch them out of my hand.
John 10:28

Look to the Lord **and his strength**; seek his face always.
1 Chronicles 16:11

Let him who does wrong continue to do wrong; let him who is vile continue to be vile; let him who does right **continue to do right**; and let him who is holy continue to be holy.
Revelation 22:11

All men will hate you because of me, but **he who stands firm** to the end will be saved.
Matthew 10:22

The path of the righteous is like the first gleam of dawn, **shining ever brighter** till the full light of day.
Proverbs 4:18

I am the vine; you are the branches. If a man remains in me and I in him, he will bear much fruit; **apart from me** you can do nothing.
John 15:5

Therefore, my dear brothers, stand firm. **Let nothing move you.** Always give yourselves fully to the work of the Lord, because you know that your labor in the Lord is not in vain.
1 Corinthians 15:58

But as for you, **continue** in what you have learned and have become convinced of, because you know those from whom you learned it.
2 Timothy 3:14

If you continue in your faith, established and firm, **not moved from the hope** held out in the gospel. This is the gospel that you heard and that has been proclaimed to every creature under heaven, and of which I, Paul, have become a servant.
Colossians 1:23

Perseverance must finish its work so that you may be mature and complete, not lacking anything.
James 1:4

DON'T BE AFRAID TO WAIT ON GOD

JFK AIRPORT

Take Jamaica
Center E to
Sutphin Blvd-
Archer Av/JFK
for ✈ AIRTF

Our culture does not value waiting. If our fast food isn't fast enough we whine and complain. If a show or movie doesn't start on time we get furious. Traffic jams ruin our day. Needless to say, patience is not a virtue practiced by most of the people in our world.

Are you guilty of wanting immediate satisfaction?

You know what you want and you want it now.

Truth be told, this attitude can actually be a positive thing in some parts of your life. But this perspective is deadly to your walk with Christ.

When was the last time you waited for God? When was the last time you needed something—whether it was an answer to a question, a material or physical need, or simply a request for God's intervention—and you waited for it. Do you make it a habit to wait prayerfully for God to answer you?

Have you ever waited for days? Weeks? Months? Years?

Or did you just give up?

See, waiting on God is a kind of perseverance, too. When you wait on God, you are persevering while a need goes unmet. You are trusting that God can and will meet your need in His own time, in His own way, and that His way will be the right way.

You are trusting that His way will be worth the wait.

Don't get caught up in the immediate-satisfaction mentality. Not in life, and especially not in your faith. God doesn't work on our timetable. And by waiting on Him we actually stand to learn much, much more about Him, ourselves, our faith, and even our needs.

Don't be afraid to wait on God.

If it feels like at times you are all alone, if it seems like it's "you against the world" and the world is winning, if it looks like you're the only one standing up for something worth fighting for, here's some good news:

You're not alone!

God promised to be with you always. And He is. God sent His Word to give you encouragement, knowledge, and support. The Holy Spirit lives in you and empowers you to stay strong. The Church, the worldwide collection of all people who believe in and serve Jesus, is alive and active on this earth, waiting to help you.

See, you aren't alone. Don't be afraid to take a stand.

MOSES & JOSHUA

OK, it's Bible Story 101. Time to test your knowledge.

What do you remember about Moses and his story? Write down a summary below:

Second question: What do remember about Joshua and his story? Write down all you recall in the space below:

Here's a recap. Moses was God's handpicked leader to free His people from slavery in Egypt. Moses was a just and faithful leader. But due to the people's sin along the journey from Egypt to the promised land, God told Moses that he would never actually enter the land. Next up: Joshua. Joshua was Moses' right-hand man. He had been at Moses' side while Moses was leading the people. Joshua was the heir to the leadership of the Israelites.

Now, take a moment and read Joshua 1:1–9. But before you do, here's some quick background info. Moses had died and Joshua was about to take over leadership of God's people. Before he did, God had some words of encouragement. As you read the passage, pay close attention to verse 5.

What important message did God give Joshua?

If you were in Joshua's shoes, how would this make you feel?

You could spend hours reading about all the ways God was with Moses. And here God was telling Joshua, "You know what? All the awesome stuff I did for Moses? I'm going to do the same for you." What a powerful promise! It must have been just what Joshua needed to get ready to lead God's people.

The important truth is this: God does not call His people to a task without empowering them. God calls you *then* gives you His strength to carry out the call. As you live out your call, don't forget Joshua and how God promised to be with him.

LIFE IS FULL OF CHALLENGES.
REMEMBER, YOU ARE
NEVER
ALONE.
GOD IS WITH YOU.
ALWAYS.

reverb
reverb
reverb
310

FLAMMABLE LIQU

REFLECTION

There comes a time in any journey where you reach the end. When you arrive at this point, it's always a good idea to turn around and see where you've been. **This is your chance to do that.**

During the course of this book, you've had the opportunity to learn a lot about God and His mission for the world. And you've learned so much about how your participation in that mission affects you and the world around you.

Here's an opportunity for you to think back on where you've been. Below you will find the chapters of the book listed along with space for you to write. Think back over the specific chapters and recall any significant lessons you might have learned. And if you want, write down any thoughts. If not, just thumb back through the book and recall any activities that catch your eye.

This is for your benefit only. So, take a moment and reflect on where God has taken you.

DRIVE

EMPOWERED

STEP OUT

CRUX

THE ANSWER

LIVING LOUD

TRANSFER

SQUEEZE

Just like He promised Joshua, God will never leave you alone. He will not forget about you either. He has taken you through this journey, teaching you so much about Himself and about you. He will use the person you now are to achieve His purposes in this world. Spend some time thanking Him for the work He has done in your life, as well as for His faithfulness in using you for His glory.

THE LORD IS MY ROCK,
MY FORTRESS,
AND MY SAVIOR;
MY GOD IS MY ROCK, IN WHOM I FIND PROTECTION

HE IS MY SHIELD, THE POWER
THAT SAVES ME, AND MY PLACE OF SAFETY.

HE IS MY REFUGE, MY SAVIOR,
THE ONE WHO SAVES ME FROM VIOLENCE

I CALLED ON THE LORD
WHO IS WORTHY OF PRAISE,
AND HE SAVED ME FROM MY
ENEMIES

- 2 Samuel 22:2

YOUR COMMISSION

Before Joshua could lead the people to the land God had promised them, he needed a holy nudge . . . a not-so-subtle reminder that he was not alone.

Joshua had a task. And God took the chance to tell Joshua exactly how He would be with him to accomplish the task.

God said:
Have I not commanded you? Be strong and courageous. Do not be terrified; do not be discouraged, for the Lord your God will be with you wherever you go.

The same God that was with Joshua is with you.

God called Joshua to a task. God calls YOU to a task.

God wanted Joshua to introduce His people to their land inheritance. God wants YOU to introduce people to Him, their spiritual inheritance.

God promised to be with Joshua as he lived out the call. And God promises to be with YOU as you do the same.

So . . . go. Go out into the world. Go out into the world as a difference-maker, taking the hope of Jesus Christ to a world that needs hope. Do not fear, do not hesitate, do not question your potential, and do not second-guess your role. God has chosen YOU to be a part of making His name known throughout the entire world.

Do not delay. Use your life to make a radical difference . . . and start today!

So here you are.

Your journey is over. You've arrived at the end of this book.

There's an interesting question you should probably consider. Ready? Here it goes:

Are you different now than you were before you started this book?

It's a fair question. After all, you've invested a great deal of your time in reading and working through this book.

Do you know more about God's mission and plan for this world than you did before you started?

Do you have a greater idea of your role in His plan?

Are you excited about taking part in His mission of love for the world?

Do you feel more equipped to encounter those who might not know Christ?

Hopefully, you answered "yes" to the questions above. Hopefully, you're already making a difference for Christ in this world.

The most important thing you should have gathered from your time spent in this book is that God's plan includes you. God planned to use you to be His voice on this earth. He expects it from you. He desires it from you. He wants you to be a part of what He is doing.

Don't miss out on the chance to make your life count. Don't miss the opportunity to be a vital part of God's plan to redeem the world. Be bold. Commit to following Christ. Commit to allowing Him to use your life as a tool to reach the world.

And don't wait. Because God's mission won't wait on you.

OUR LIVES ECHO IN THE WORLD

ACKNOWLEDGMENTS

EXECUTIVE EDITOR
Andy Blanks

ART DIRECTOR
Brandi K. Etheredge

AUTHORS
Andy Blanks
Jeremy Maxfield

Graphic Design
Brandi K. Etheredge
Shane Etheredge
Laurel-Dawn B. McBurney
Zack Nichols
Katie Beth Shirley
Ruth Tinsley

Copy Editor
Kaci Hindman

Student Life Creative Team
Becca Davis
Brandi K. Etheredge
Monte Erwin
Drew Francis
Amy Harlan
Chris Kinsley
Jeremy Maxfield
Erin Moon
Taylor Robinson

OTHER 31 Verses Devotional Journals

IDENTITY

EVERY TEENAGER SHOULD KNOW

THE WAY

CHRIST

THE BIBLE

FL!P

Here & Now